AWESOME CLAIMS
CUSTOMER SERVICE

PART 1

BY **CARL VAN**
AND **JON COSCIA**

INTERNATIONAL INSURANCE INSTITUTE, INC.

Written by Carl van Lamsweerde and Jon Coscia

Contributions by Jim Wilson

Edited by Jim Wilson and Greg Larman
Additional Edits by Lisa Ferrier and Karla Alcerro

First Edition

Copyright ©2020 International Insurance Institute, Inc.
6221 S. Claiborne Ave. Ste. 639
New Orleans, LA 70125
T: 504-393-4570

www.InsuranceInstitute.com

All rights reserved. Published by International Insurance Institute, Inc.
ISBN: 979-8-6303-4985-9
Printed in Charleston, SC.

AWESOME CLAIMS CUSTOMER SERVICE

PART 1

BY CARL VAN
(Author of <u>The 8 Characteristics of the Awesome Adjuster</u> and <u>The Claims Cookbook</u>)

AND JON COSCIA
(President of Latitude Subrogation Services)

DEDICATION

We would like to dedicate this book to Brad Schram, a person of enormous character.

He is a leader in his community, a friend and a partner. His work ethic, family values and loyalty are extraordinary and plays a part in everything he does.

He is caring, appreciative, and most of all supportive.

We are both indebted to Brad for his financial generosity, his perceptiveness and his honesty.

ACKNOWLEDGEMENTS

Without the support of some key customers, we would never have had the time or opportunity to write this book. We'd like to take the time to thank these especially loyal customers for their extraordinary support.

Jeff Suloff – Mountain West Mutual

Evelyn Jorgensen – Selective Insurance

Jon Medel, Evan Di Bella - Northbridge Insurance

Lyn Schriver and Shawn Knauts – Shelter Insurance

Diann Cohen – Macro-Pro

Debra Hinz – Executives in Workers' Compensation

Don Simon and Roger Graff – Michigan Farm Bureau

Bob Cretel, Amanda Escamilla, Claudia Rodriguez and Mary Weddle – Automobile Clubs

AWESOME CLAIMS CUSTOMER SERVICE

Dale Silvey, Stephen Mundt and Tom Vitale – American Family Insurance

Ken Bunn – Builders Mutual

Toni Clark and Melanie Royale – Hallmark Insurance

Ben Ebling and Paul Webb – Latitude Subrogation Services

Teresa Hamm and Lyndon Friesen – Red River Mutual

Belkys Stallings – Security First

Mary Bruggeman – Great American

Jeff Gagnon, Brittany Noble and Maggie Cain – AMICA

Carmen Sharp – Hanover Insurance

Stephanie Jackson – Louisiana Citizens Property

Anthony Valente – Legacy Insurance

Paul Becker – Hastings Mutual

Michelle Piracci – Universal Property

Jeff Kuss and Patty Herbert – Accident Fund

Stacy Hosman – Hosman & Associates

Kevin McKenzie and Cole Brown – Arkansas Farm Bureau

Extra Thanks:

James Wilds – Frankenmuth Mutual - Without Jim's willingness to take a chance on Latitude, Latitude would not have turned into the company it is today, 23 years later, over 100 employees strong and growing, still representing the same core values all these years later.

Gordon Gingrich – Pioneer State Mutual - For always having encouraging words, believing in our business partnership and never forgetting our humble roots. It is an honor to know a man of such integrity.

Sharon Carruth – Hanover – For believing in Jon and standing by his side.

Glenn Shapiro – Allstate Insurance – For allowing us to use him as an example of what it takes to be an extraordinary leader. He is personable, knowledgeable and accessible, and has been the subject of many of our articles and workshops on Effective Leadership.

OUR THANKS

Thanks

Thanks to our children and grandchildren *Amanda, Molly, Layne, Lillie, Jack, Jake, Vivian and Evelyn* for bringing so much joy into our lives.

Thanks to our friends *Jim Wilson, Greg Larman, Lisa Ferrier and Karla Alcerro.* who helped edit this book and bring it to life.

Special Thanks

Special thanks to our wives *Ann and Ivy* for all of their love and support.

Very Special Thanks

Very special thanks to *Brad Schram* who has provided career opportunities and financial support to both of us, allowing us the freedom to write this book.

ABOUT THE AUTHORS

Carl Van was born Carl Christian Gregory Maria Baron van Lamsweerde. He was the second son of a prominent Dutch noble and artist, Franciscus Ludovicus Aloysius Maria Baron van Lamsweerde.

After the death of Carl's father at the age of 11, his mother, Joyce, married John E. Martin. Mr. Martin was a successful business owner and investor. Mr. Martin had tremendous influence over Carl, recapping stories of coming to America with virtually nothing and building a successful business. Carl admired his new father greatly and marveled at his generosity.

Carl had a remarkable resemblance to his father Franz and was greatly influenced by John. His mother would often comment, "I look at Carl and I see Franz. Then he starts to talk, and out comes John."

Carl worked his way through college, taking years of night school to earn his degree in Insurance. By the time he earned his degree, Carl was already a Regional Claims Manager, and even writing and teaching several IEA courses.

With his first marriage came his daughter Amanda Elaine Denise Baroness van Lamsweerde, who Carl continuously proclaims is a child genius.

Carl married Ann Elizabeth Wimsatt, on July 16, 1994, and together they have lived in Sacramento, CA, Nashville, TN, and now reside in New Orleans, LA. In April of 1998, Carl sold his house, cashed in his retirement, and gambled it all on the idea that insurance companies would be interested in meaningful, real-life claims training. He created International Insurance Institute, Inc. a company dedicated to the enhancement of the insurance claims industry, and now widely considered the single best claims training company in the United States and Canada.

Carl Van has dedicated his life to studying how people think and interact and has developed classes and programs to improve the success of individuals as well as business groups.

I have known Carl since we met in kindergarten, and even back then in our school days. Carl looked out for people. Obviously, Carl was honing his skills that he uses today. It only takes a few minutes in his presence to know how passionately he believes that the greatest thing a person can do in this life, is be of service to someone in need. That, he insists, is the opportunity most of us have every single day.

CARL VAN AND JON COSCIA

In this book, Carl shares his wit, wisdom, knowledge and sixth sense of dealing with people. He's a great friend and an inspiration. I hope you find this book as valuable in your world as Carl has been in mine.

—Steve Belkin, Open All Nite Entertainment.

AWESOME CLAIMS CUSTOMER SERVICE

Jon Keith Coscia was born in the Borough of Westwood, New Jersey to Charles Martin Coscia and Alicia Louise Mitchell whom married and had 10 children. Jon, who is the first-born son, has been very fortunate to have had a wonderful upbringing within a kind and loving family. Growing up with such a large dynamic family has helped shape him into the man he has become today. Having a brother, Anthony, with CP (Cerebral Palsy), Jon has clearly seen the day to day struggles that others can easily take for granted. Anthony has instilled in Jon the appreciation for a strong work-ethic, kindness for others, and compassion.

Jon is the consummate entrepreneur. At age 12 he negotiated the purchase from his neighborhood friend the rights to take over the local newspaper route to add to his existing route. He started his work life off handling these two paper routes which carried him onward through high school. After graduating, Jon was hired as a Manager at Bill Knapp's Restaurant. There he met his future wife, Ivy. Twenty-eight happy years later, they have three fabulous children, Jake Douglas, Vivian Rose and Evelyn Jane. His family gives Jon the joys of life that storybooks and fairytales have been written about.

Jon went on to form many small business ventures as an entrepreneur and has held several managerial, consulting, and C-level positions within the insurance industry. Jon is a founding member of Latitude Subrogation Services where he has been able to plant his inspired roots and grow both personally and professionally while helping others grow along the way. Jon is passionate about paying it forward and sharing his knowledge; a true mark of a great leader.

I'm proud to have known Jon for 27 years, been his best man at his wedding, and a godfather to his son. Having access to his expertise has been invaluable.

—Timothy P. Herndon, President/CEO, Herndon & Associates

PROFESSIONAL CAREERS

Carl Van, ITP, President & CEO of International Insurance Institute, Inc., graduated from California State University, Sacramento where he received his bachelor's degree in Insurance. He has been in the insurance claims industry since 1980 and has held the positions of Claims Adjuster, Claims Supervisor, Claims Manager, Division Claims Manager and Regional Manager over Claims, Loss Control and Premium Audit.

Mr. Van has set up 5 in-house claims training programs for various insurance companies throughout the United States, and has written articles for Claims magazine, Claims Education Magazine, Claims Advisor, Claims People magazine, The Subrogator, The National Underwriter, California Insurance Journal and has been published in over 100 other magazines. He is the author of over 75 technical and soft skill workshops being taught throughout the U.S., Canada and the U.K.

He has been a keynote speaker at claims conferences around the country, a trainer at an international U.S-Japanese executive training program, a guest speaker at hundreds of claims association seminars, and selected as the opening presenter at some of the most prestigious claims conferences in the United States, Canada and Australia.

Mr. Van is the Dean of the School of Claims Performance and has served as both board member and Regional Vice President of the Society of Insurance Trainers and Educators where he earned his ITP designation (Insurance Training Professional).

He is owner and publisher of Claims Education Magazine, and board president of the Claims Education Conference.

Mr. Van is creator, presenter and producer of all claims training videos at Claims Education On-Line, which include Time Management, Customer Service, Negotiations and Critical Thinking, all specific to claims professionals.

He is the owner and publisher of Claims Professional Books On Line, and is the author of the highly acclaimed book *The 8 Characteristics of the Awesome Adjuster*, which has sold internationally throughout the United States, Canada, Guam, Singapore, France, Australia, England, Chile, Ireland, and 25 other countries. Other books by Carl Van include *Gaining Cooperation, Gaining Cooperation for the Workers' Comp. Professional, The*

Claims Cookbook, Attitude, Ability and the 80/20 Rule, Negotiation Skills for the Claims Professional and *The Eight Characteristics of the Awesome Employee.*

Mr. Van writes all materials for his *Carl Van Claims Expert* blog and provides claims tips on his *Carl Van Professional Speaker* You Tube channel.

Mr. Van writes all the lyrics for all songs performed by Carl Van and the Awesome Adjuster Band, including all 11 songs on their CD "I'm a Claims Man."

Other credits include being an arbitrator, a licensed agent, a TASA expert witness for insurance Bad Faith suits, as well as a national auditor for a federal regulatory agency.

www.InsuranceInstitute.com

www.ClaimsEducationConference.net

www.CarlVan.org

www.ClaimsEducationMagazine.com

www.ClaimsMusic.com

www.Facebook.com/CarlVanSpeaker

AWESOME CLAIMS CUSTOMER SERVICE

www.ClaimsEducationOnLine.com

www.Twitter.com/CarlVanSpeaker

www.ClaimsProfessionalBooks.com

www.Linkedin.com (Carl Van – Awesome Adjuster group)

www.YouTube.com/CarlVanTV

www.CarlVanClaimsExpert.wordpress.com

Jon Coscia, CSRP, President of Latitude Subrogation Services, holds an Associate Degree in Criminal Justice from Schoolcraft College, MI and a Certified Subrogation Recovery Professional designation from the National Association of Subrogation Professionals.

He has held the positions of Claims Adjuster, Claims Supervisor and Claims Manager with a national insurance carrier, and brings with him over 23 years of subrogation, claims management and leadership experience.

Mr. Coscia currently oversees all areas of company operations including sales and marketing, strategic planning, accounting, business unit operations, claims, information technology, human resources and employee development.

He is currently an active Board member of National Association of Subrogation Professionals and current member of the Property and Liability Resource Bureau and the National Association of Insurance Companies.

www.Latitudesubro.com

www.Linkedin.com/in/joncoscia/

INSPIRATION FOR THE BOOK

By Carl Van

"Howdy." That's how Mike greeted everyone he knew, and sometimes people he didn't know.

During the course of my claims career, I have had the opportunity to work with some truly exceptional people. Mike Noakes was one of them.

Mike Noakes joined the insurance claims industry in 1980 as a claims adjuster trainee at Progressive Insurance. Through the years, he moved up the ranks to claims supervisor, claims manager and regional manager.

Mike continued to turn down numerous high-level positions in other locations of the country, choosing to stay in the Sacramento area because he wanted a stable family and church life.

AWESOME CLAIMS CUSTOMER SERVICE

Mike hired me as a claims adjuster many years ago, and I had the honor of working for him during a period of growth at our company.

As my manager, Mike showed extraordinary concern for his employees and his customers. He was respected for his knowledge of course, but his commitment to the people around him was his most profound leadership quality. More than anything else, Mike was known as a remarkable mentor to anyone who wanted to improve and do his or her best. He used to tell aspiring managers, "Be proactive. Think like an owner."

Mike was the first to promote me into claims management. Working alongside Mike, I was constantly impressed with how he inspired people to do their best.

As I grew to know Mike over the years, I found him to be an incredibly dedicated family man, as well as a respected leader in his church. Mike married his wife Sheila on February 3, 1977. Together they had three children, Shelby, Chad, and Nicole. Mike of course adored his grandchildren, Halle, Cohen, James, Brady, Olivia, and Everett.

At his church, Mike served as bishop in The Church of Jesus Christ of Latter-day Saints in Rocklin, California. Mike enjoyed giving his time to helping others and held callings his entire life. He had the unique ability to make those around him feel important.

In 2002 he accepted a position with a start-up company called Esurance and was asked to build a claims department. Since its inception, Mike guided the claims organization through its expansion as its Corporate Claims Director.

Throughout his career, Mike was the recipient of many honors and awards such as Claims Manager of the Year, Best Claims Office, and many others.

A few years ago, when I was developing my theories on identifying traits that make great claims professionals, I started with two main categories: Givers and Takers. Mike was my inspiration for the Givers category.

Mike Noakes passed away on April 9, 2012, when he succumbed to Non-Hodgkin's lymphoma. The claims world certainly lost one of its best.

In 2014, we produced a music CD by <u>Carl Van and the Awesome Adjuster Band</u>. The title of the CD is "I'm a Claims Man," which is the final song on the CD. We dedicated that song to Mike as follows: "*This song is dedicated to Mike Noakes, the best claims man we've ever known.*"

AWESOME CLAIMS CUSTOMER SERVICE

Mike enjoyed playing golf, reading, and was quite proud of his guitar collection. He was kind, patient and thoughtful. The impact he had on everyone around him was truly amazing and will never be forgotten.

I will miss him terribly. I can't bring myself to say goodbye, so for now, I'll just say, "Howdy Mike."

Mike Noakes
(July 9, 1956 – April 9, 2012)

TABLE OF CONTENTS

Introduction xxxi

Chapter 1   Making the Claims Job Easier 1

Chapter 2   Taking Control 5

Chapter 3   Five Things You Need to Know 13

Chapter 4   Responding to the Snide Comment 35

Chapter 5   Gaining Cooperation 51

Chapter 6   The Empathic Connection 81

Chapter 7   Nail Down Questions 93

Chapter 8   The Voice Mail Multiplier 113

Chapter 9   Overcoming the Question after Question Cycle 127

Chapter 10 The Five Standards for Great Claims Customer Service 151

Chapter 11 Active Listening 161

Chapter 12 Dealing with the Angry Customer · · · · · 181

Chapter 13 The Opportunity to Help People · · · · · · 201

Chapter 14 Changing Carl's Attitude · · · · · · · · · · · · 221

Chapter 15 Telephone Techniques to Avoid · · · · · · · 227

Chapter 16 Claims is a Customer Service Business · · 235

Professional Speaking Services · · · · · · · · · · · · · · · · · 239

In-Person Training Services · · · · · · · · · · · · · · · · · · · 243

On-Line Training Services · 247

Educational Articles by Carl Van · · · · · · · · · · · · · · · 249

Articles Featuring Carl Van · · · · · · · · · · · · · · · · · · · 257

Additional Books by Carl Van · · · · · · · · · · · · · · · · · 261

Contact Carl Van · 263

Frequently Asked Questions · · · · · · · · · · · · · · · · · · · 265

INTRODUCTION

International Insurance Institute, Inc. was started in March of 1998. From the very beginning, the <u>Awesome Claims Customer Service</u> course was one of the most popular workshops. The fact that solid customer service is a critical skill in claims is understood by almost everyone in the insurance industry.

Now, 22 years later, the <u>Awesome Claims Customer Service</u> course is the most popular workshop, with over 130,000 students completing the course to date. The <u>Negotiation Skills for Claims Professional</u> course is a close second with 110,000 students.

Although most of the concepts in this book are from models that were developed for the in-person workshop, we will do our best to convert them here.

As with many of Carl's other books, there are going to be concepts and ideas that cross over from book to book. You may read something in here and recognize the concept from another one of Carl's books. That is simply because the concepts we hold most true, like treating people well, cross over the different subjects so easily.

You should know that we did not conduct formal research. We have no control groups to test out the theories and no written documentation to substantiate each and every hypothesis. What we do offer is practical experience and examples to better illustrate how to deliver superior customer service in claims.

CHAPTER 1

Making the Claims Job Easier

Claims is a different business than most businesses. In claims, our customers have had something bad happen to them. They didn't want it, they didn't ask for it, and they don't like it. So sometimes we have to deal with our customers a little bit differently. We get calls from clients quite a bit asking, "Hey, can you deliver a class on how to be more empathetic? We want our claims people to learn how to be friendlier. We want them to be more polite." This, of course, is fine but this isn't a book on politeness. We promise you we won't be teaching you how to say, "Hello, my name is Carl Van and I'll be denying your claim today."

AWESOME CLAIMS CUSTOMER SERVICE

One time we did, however, receive a call from a client who said, "We want a class on how to teach our claims people to make their job easier." Ahh... now *this* is what we're interested in. Making your claims job easier is what this book is all about and showing you ways to enhance your customer service skills is the tool we use to achieve this goal.

Want to make your job easier? Then improve your customer service skills. Want to improve your customer service skills? Then make your job easier. Virtually everything you do in order to make your job easier does improve customer service. Even those things we mentioned before, being friendly, being polite, being empathetic, are important parts of customer service as you will see.

If after reading this book you can get customers to listen to you better, remember more of what you said, be more patient, be much more reasonable, stop calling as much, trust you more, be up front about what it is they want, cooperate much more, and understand you better, would that be a few hours well spent? Well, that's it. That's the outline for this book. We're going to cover every one of these topics. But at every turn, we're going to be talking about the impact of customer service. If we accomplish all of these goals, we will greatly improve customer service, increase retention, and make our jobs much, much, easier in the process. So, let's get started.

CHAPTER 2

Taking Control

If you were asked to complete this sentence, "My job as a claims professional would be so much easier if the customers would just _____," what would you say? Think about it for a moment. Usually, when we ask claim professionals this question, we get answers like *listen, remember, be patient, be reasonable, stop calling, trust me, just tell us what they want, cooperate,* and *understand* to name a few.

As a claims professional, do you have any control over whether or not someone is listening to you at any time? Well, yes, you have tremendous control. If you think you don't have control over whether or not someone is listening, then you probably have been working much too hard. While the point of this book is to improve customer service skills, doing so will also make the claims job easier. Would it make your job easier if you learned how to make people listen to you? Would it also make your job easier if you learned how to avoid doing those things that stop people from listening? Improving your customer service skills will help you accomplish both of these goals.

As a claims professional, do you have any control over whether or not people remember what you say? Again, the answer is yes. Right now, we present information in a way which tends to result in people remembering only about 20 percent of what we say. How many times have you provided a certain amount of information to a customer just to have them turn around and ask you questions? What do they usually ask about? They ask about what you just said. So, what do you do? You answer the questions, and what do they do? They ask more questions, and what do you do? You answer them, and now, you're playing ping-pong back and forth. What if there was a way to increase the 20 percent people remember to 60 or 70 percent? Would that be valuable for you? Would that make your job a little bit easier?

As a claims professional, do you have any control over whether or not people are patient? Well, you certainly can't make someone be patient. However, in claims, we often do or say things that cause people to become impatient. Do you have any control over whether or not people are reasonable? Again, you can't make someone be reasonable. Nevertheless, there are some very common phrases we use and things we do in claims that tend to create unreasonableness.

Before we continue, here's a quick example of how we might make a customer unreasonable. When we are monitoring phone calls, we often hear claims people basically say the worst thing you can say. They will say things like, "Mr. Insured, I know you want your entire roof replaced, but you only had a few shingles damaged. Now, you are going to have to be reasonable." Or, "Mr. Insured, I know you want $60 a day for home health care but your policy only allows $15 a day. Now, you need to be reasonable." We say things like this in order to get the customer to be reasonable but here's what we want you to think about. As soon as you tell someone they are going to have to do anything, what automatically goes through their mind? "I don't have to do anything."

As a matter of fact, you have planted a seed in their mind that whatever you ask them to do, they won't like it. Also, when you tell someone they are going to have to be reasonable, what did you just call them? Exactly! You have called them *unreasonable*. With the goal of getting them to change their mind, you've just called them a name. You know the type of response you are going to receive from a customer most of the time when you tell them they are not being reasonable. Their response will be, "I *am* being reasonable." Now you have the customer admitting if they change their mind, they have been an unreasonable person. Can you make someone be reasonable? No, but you have a tremendous influence over whether or not they will be reasonable by the things you say and do.

Do we have any control over how often a customer calls? Well, you do have a great deal of control over this. There are certain things we say in claims that tend to make people call us. We don't realize we're doing it, because we don't fully appreciate the impact of the words and phrases we use.

Do you have any control over whether our customers trust us? Well, believe it or not, we have tremendous influence over whether or not people trust us. In claims, we use a wide variety of words and phrases most psychologists tell us are ways to send a message not to trust us. A good example of a phrase which might send the wrong message is *willing to*. We often say things like, "We're willing to pay you $5,000 for your auto." Or, "We're willing to pay you $5,000 for your stolen television set." The problem with the words *willing to* is that they mean, "I'd really rather not, and I wouldn't if I didn't have to, but I'm willing to." You see, that's a very different message. To tell someone that you are willing to do something tells them you don't want to do it, and you're only doing it because you're trapped. This is a very different message than, "Mr. Insured, your claim is worth up to $5,000, and I want to make sure you get everything you're entitled to." You see, there are certain ways we can say things that make people want to trust us. Unfortunately, many times we get caught up in using the wrong ones.

Do we have any control over whether the customer tells us what they want? As people who monitor phone calls for many different insurance companies in many different countries, we can tell you that most of the time, customers are telling us *exactly* what they want. Unfortunately, we're not listening. In order to deliver outstanding customer service, we need be good listeners, and we often miss the boat.

Can we make people cooperate? Would that make our job easier if we could get people to cooperate? Well, we do have a great deal of control over this as well. You can't *make* someone cooperate. However, we're going to learn a three-step process that has a tremendous impact on whether or not people *want* to cooperate. The way we get people to cooperate now often sounds like a threat or ultimatum.

Do you have any control over whether or not someone understands you? Well, hopefully they've read their

AWESOME CLAIMS CUSTOMER SERVICE

policy. Nevertheless, if customers are listening when we're talking, if they remember what we say, if they are patient enough to let us do our job, if they're in a reasonable state of mind, they trust us, and we're listening to what it is they really want, there's a very good chance they're going to understand what we have to tell them.

CHAPTER 3

Five Things You Need to Know

Improving your customer service skills will help make your claims job easier. In order to do this, it becomes vitally important to understand what makes a great customer service company truly great. There are five standards for great customer service companies. Those of us in the insurance industry can benefit from knowing them.

Why are you great?

The first standard of great customer service companies is that they know why they are great. If you ask them, they will, of course, say, "Yes, we are great." If you ask them how they know they are great, they will have the answer. Some of us don't always have that answer but it's very helpful. As a matter of fact, it's one of the five standards of great customer service companies: They know why they are great. So, take a moment, grab some paper and a pen, and write down an answer for this question: How do you know you're great at customer service? How could you tell someone that you are great at customer service and be able to explain it to them? What are your standards for that? Give yourself enough time for serious reflection.

Well, did you come up with a few? We're sure you did. We like to ask our students this question: "How do you know you're a great customer service company?" Sometimes they say, "Well, our surveys say we're great." That's good. Sometimes they will say, "Well, we don't get any complaint calls." That's good too but, in this case, be careful. If you judge yourself by the lack of a negative, you might be shooting for mediocrity. Not having complaint calls doesn't mean you're great; it means you might not be a disaster.

Here's an example of what we mean. Jon has a friend who is an airline pilot. Let's say Jon comes up to him and says, "Hey Ben, you're an airline pilot, right?"

"Yeah."

"Are you any good?"

"Yeah, I'm great."

"Well, how do you know you're any good?"

"Well, I haven't crashed this month."

Is Ben a good pilot because he hasn't had a crash? Well, he's not a disaster. However, we're not so sure that's a good standard for him to say he's a great pilot. In claims, if we say we're good at customer service because we don't have any complaints that can be a dangerous standard. We're shooting for mediocrity. We've got to shoot much higher than that. So again, how do you know you're any good? That's the question.

The answer for us in claims is *retention*. Customer service for us in claims and in the insurance business, in general, is retention. We know we're a great customer service company because we have a great retention rate. We, in the insurance industry, know that retention is critical for us. It's not free money, but it's almost free. We've already done the marketing. We've already done the advertising. Now, all we need to do is what? Hold on to people, right? So, we have to know that in claims, retention is an indicator we've done a great job in customer service.

So, knowing why you are a great customer service company is the first standard.

Where do you stand?

The second standard of great customer service companies is they know where they stand. Now that you know *why* you are a great customer service company; you must now know where you stand. What is the retention rate at your company? Do you know what it is? It's OK if you don't. Most claims people don't. Think about this: If it's one of the standards for great customer service companies, shouldn't we know? That's one of the things which separate great customer service companies from everybody else. They know exactly why they're great, and they know exactly where they stand. In claims, we often don't know our retention rate.

Here's an example. Let's say you go up to an NBA player and you ask, "Are you good? Are you great?"

"Yeah, I'm great. I'm one of the best there is."

"How do you know?"

"Because of how many points I score per game. I've got a great average per game."

"Really...Well what's your average?"

"I don't know."

Well, how can you say you're great if you don't know if you're meeting your standard for greatness? Because the insurance industry standard for great customer service is retention rate, you must know whether your company's retention rate meets the standard for great customer service. So, knowing where you stand in customer service is the second standard, and we hope you keep this in mind.

Where are you going?

The third standard of great customer service companies is they know where they are going. Everybody in a great customer service company knows why they're great, where they stand, and where they are going. So, we will ask you another question: What is your company's stated goal for retention rate in the coming year? What is it? Do you know? Again, it's OK if you don't, but knowing your company's retention rate goal is one of the things that separate great customer service companies from everybody else. They know why they are great; they know where they stand, and they know where they are going.

AWESOME CLAIMS CUSTOMER SERVICE

What is your job?

That leads us into the fourth standard of great customer service companies. The fourth standard is that people can accurately describe their job. Now we know this is going to seem odd, but this is one of the most important standards. Let's say Jon didn't know anything about claims and came up to you and said, "Hmmm...I don't know what a claims person does. Can you describe your job for me?" What are some things you do during the day? What would you say? We want you to do this. Take a few moments and write down the things you do during the day. We know you are going to say things like, "I answer the phone." That's fine. We want a nice long list. Go ahead and get started.

What did you come up with? Our students usually come up with things like *do diary, write estimates, file arbitration, answer emails,* etc. We could go on forever. Did you write down *provide customer service*? Hopefully, you did but you may not have. Many people don't. Often, we are so focused on our tasks we forget what our job is. Here's what we want you to think about. In claims, we are a customer service business. This is what we do. This is *all* we do. We don't actually *do* anything other than provide customer service.

Do we mend people's wounds when they are injured? Do we rebuild their houses? Do we fix their cars? We don't do any of these things. We arrange for those things to happen and that's the customer service piece. Sometimes we tell them, "We're not paying you anything and here's why." That's still customer service. We don't do *anything* other than provide customer service in claims. This is an accurate description of our job. What are all these other things we wrote down? They are just tasks. They're just things we have to do in order to accomplish our job. These things aren't our job. Our job is to provide customer service. And whatever it takes to provide that customer service falls under our job responsibilities.

Let's look at another example. Remember Jon's friend, Ben, the airline pilot? Let's go back to him. Let's say Jon comes up to Ben and says, "Hey Ben, you're an airline pilot, right?" and he replies, "Yeah." Jon then asks, "Well, can you describe your job? Can you tell me what an airline pilot does?" and he says, "Yeah. My job is to lift the flaps. It's to turn left. It's to turn right. It's to put down the landing gear. It's to talk on the walkie-talkie. It's to pressurize the cabin. It's to tell the flight attendants to sit down," and he goes on and on and on. Wouldn't we have to stop him? Is Ben doing a good job of accurately describing his job? No. What are all of these things he's giving Jon? Tasks—these are things he has to do. His job is much more important, much more sophisticated, much more complicated than a list of tasks. What is Ben's job as an airline pilot? His job is to fly the plane, from here to there—and not crash the plane if either of us is on it as a personal favor. What are all these other things he's telling Jon? They're tasks.

In claims, our job is much more complicated, sophisticated, and important than the list of our tasks. Our job is to provide customer service. We don't actually do anything other than provide customer service. Yet often when we ask claims people to describe their jobs, what we get is a list of their tasks.

One of our favorite movies is *Clock Watchers*. It stars Lisa Kudrow and Toni Collette. If you have a chance to rent it, by all means, do so. It's a great movie. *Clock Watchers* starts with a scene we just love. The scene begins with a customer standing in front of a receptionist, who is flipping through a magazine. A clock ticks in the background. You don't really know what's going on until the clock appears and sure enough, it's 8:59. As soon as the clock turns to exactly 9:00, the receptionist closes his magazine, acknowledges the customer, and says, "Can I help you?" It's a great scene. Is this person a good employee? Carl often ask this question of his students, and their answers might surprise you. He gets answers like, "No, he's not a good employee." "Well why?" "Well, because he should have helped the customer." "But you don't know what his job is." "Well, he shouldn't ignore the customer." "Yes, but you don't know what his job is."

Finally, someone will say, "It doesn't matter what his job is." There you go—it *does* matter what his job is. Do you know what he was told his job is when he got hired? You be here at 9:00. You leave at 5:00. Never come in late. Never leave early. Always smile when you look at the customer. Isn't he doing his job? He's doing everything his company has asked him to do. How can you say he's not a good employee? How would you feel if after six months you did every single thing your company asked you to do and at the end they say, "You know, you're not a very good employee." You'd feel pretty bad. Well, he's doing every single thing his company has asked him to do. Why isn't he a good employee? Well, he's just fine. This isn't an employee failure. This is a training failure. Someone hasn't taught him he's in the customer service business. Had someone taught him he's in the customer service business, he would be doing whatever it takes. He's not going to do anything more but that's fine.

We will actually hire an employee like this receptionist because we would rather have someone who does exactly what they think their job is over someone who doesn't give a damn, any day of the week. All we have to do is change his focus. All we have to do is teach him he's in the customer service business and he will do whatever it takes to meet that goal. But he does have one problem and that problem is he can't accurately describe his job. If we ask him to describe his job, he will say, "I sit at a desk, I answer the phones, I greet customers." He will give you a list of his tasks. What he won't say is, "I provide customer service." Again, that's a training issue more than an employee issue.

In claims, we are in a customer service business. We're in a customer service environment. Yet many times when claims people are asked to describe their job, the words *customer service* aren't even mentioned. We understand intuitively that it's part of our job. But one of the standards for great customer service companies is that every single person in the company describes their job in terms of customer service. If you ask them, "What is your job?" their first answer is, "I provide customer service." Then they will give you a list of the tasks. "I provide customer service by answering the phone. I provide customer service by installing cable. I provide customer service by cleaning this, whatever it is." Their first answer is, "I provide customer service." Then they will give you a list of their tasks. This is something that in claims, we need to learn how to do. Why? Because we don't do anything other than provide customer service. We need to have that focus. And by the way, if we have that focus, it's going to make our job much, much, easier.

What is customer service?

The fifth standard, and most important, is that great customer service companies know what customer service is. It seems like an odd standard but it's the most important. Great customer service companies know what customer service is. If you go to a group of people in that company and ask, "What is customer service?" they have all got the answer. So now we want to give you a chance. Here's what we'd like you to do. On your piece of paper, we want you to finish this sentence: Great customer service is _____. You can write anything you want. It could be a list. It could be a sentence. Write down whatever it is you think great customer service is. Take some time to give this some serious thought.

We're sure you've come up with a good list. Things we hear quite a bit are customer service is meeting the customer's desires, meeting the customer's wants, being empathetic, treating customers like you would want to be treated (the Golden Rule), and listening. These are all great answers. In claims, we want to give you a very specific and precise answer that should make your job much easier. Customer service is meeting or exceeding the customer's expectations. Meeting or exceeding customer expectations is key for us. It's not just meeting their wants or desires. It's meeting or exceeding their expectations. Here's an example of what we mean. We said that one of our standards for great customer service companies is that they have a high retention rate. We also said that you need know where you stand. And no doubt at least some of us admit we don't know where we stand. Whatever your retention rate happens to be—and it doesn't matter much what it is, whether it's 85 or 90 percent, it doesn't much matter—whatever it is, this retention rate is a mixed bag. This includes people who have claims, but also the people who haven't had claims. Your retention rate includes people you've retained just because they get a bill, but there is another retention rate which only includes people who have had claims. It represents only that group of people. Would you imagine the retention rate of only the people who have had claims would be higher or lower than the normal retention rate? Well, believe it or not, industry wide, it's lower. Why would people leave us after they experienced the very thing we sell, which is customer service?

It has been said that the people that leave an insurance company after a claim, 25 percent leave because they are worried about their rates going up, or they weren't happy with what they got paid. The other 75 percent will leave because of the way they *feel* they were treated. Not the way they *were* treated; the way they *feel* they were treated. You see, it's not the service you're delivering; it's the service you're delivering in comparison to their expectations which is important. If you meet or exceed someone's expectation, they will probably stay with you. If you fall short of those expectations, they will probably leave you.

In claims we have the opportunity to set people's expectations and we don't take it. It's the key to customer service and the key to making your job easier. Let us share with you a true story. Carl was monitoring a phone call at an insurance company in a claims operation and an insurance adjuster received a call from a customer who was upset because of something which occurred at the body shop. The adjuster responded to the customer by saying, "I'll tell you what sir, let me go ahead and call the body shop and I'll call you right back, OK?" The customer replied, "Yeah, great, that's fine." So, the adjuster hangs up and calls the body shop. Now let us ask you a question right now: What is the customer's expectation of when they are going to get a call back, given the fact that the adjuster just said, "I'll call you right back?" How long? Five minutes? Ten minutes? Twenty minutes? Who knows? The point is, we have absolutely no idea what the customer's expectation is, yet it's the only standard for whether or not this person, this adjuster named Jake, is going to deliver great customer service.

Jake calls the body shop. It takes the body shop manager about 30 minutes to get to the phone. So, you can forget any 5 or 20 minute call back. He walks the body shop manager through the process, and you know what, we've got to tell you, if Jake was any less trained or experienced, he would have gotten snookered. But he didn't. He walks the body shop manager step-by-step through the process, and by the time he's done, he is right, and they are wrong. Carl was thinking, "Wow, this guy's an ace." Well, guess what? After he hangs up with the body shop manager, he calls the customer. "Yeah, this is Jake giving you a call back." About 45 minutes has elapsed so guess what the customer says? "It's about time." That's right. That's exactly what the customer said, "It's about time."

Think about this. Right now, Jake worked his heart out to deliver great customer service. Yet what was the expectation of the customer? He was going to take less time. Jake thinks he did a great job of providing great customer service. What was the customer's comment? "It's about time. What took so long?" What the customer is saying is, "You didn't meet my expectation." So, of course Jake, being a good adjuster, tries to let the customer know, "Well, you know sir, it takes a while. I had to get the body shop manager on the phone." Of course, now he's just giving a bunch of excuses. So, do excuses usually calm customers down? No, they usually make customers more upset. So, the customer says, "Well, you know, if I knew it was going to take this long, I would have told you to call me at work." And Jake says, "Well, sir, I did solve your problem by the way." "Yeah, fine whatever" is the customer's response and the customer hangs up.

Allow us to ask you a question: Did Jake provide outstanding customer service? Well, he thinks he did. The customer just doesn't think so because his expectation wasn't met. Allow us to pose this question to you: What if Jake had said, "Sir, this could easily take an hour. I'm going to have to get the body shop person on the phone. We're going to have to walk through the estimate. I might have to call the adjuster who wrote the estimate. This could even take up to an hour and a half. It's 8:00 now, how about I call you back by 9:30?" and the customer says, "Fine, call me at work then." Now we call the customer 45 minutes later, at work, with the answer.

Have we provided outstanding customer service? Have we met the customer's expectation? We've actually exceeded it. We have exceeded the customer's expectation simply because we took the time to set it. Now, we have a customer that thinks they've been treated well. Seventy-five percent of the time people leave an insurance company after a claim, and it's because of the way they *feel* they were treated. We have control over this and believe it or not, it will make our job much easier. Why didn't Jake do that? Very simply, it's a training issue. Jake hadn't been trained that customer service is meeting or exceeding the customer's expectations. Had he known that; he would have taken the time to set the customer's expectation.

We said before that part of this book was to make your job easier. We also said it would be easier if customers were reasonable. We said it would be easier if customers were more patient. Well, guess what? You have tremendous control over this. A great way to get customers to be reasonable and have reasonable expectations is to set them. Set them yourself. Setting expectations is also a great way to get customers to be patient. Let them know how long something is going to take and set their expectation. We can't tell you how many times we've heard good, hard working, adjusters say things like, "OK, as soon as I get that estimate, I'll call you" or "As soon as I read that report, I'll give you a call." When? "Let me check with my supervisor and I'll get back to you." When? The problem is people are impatient and they are unreasonable often because we don't help them by setting expectations. You have tremendous control over this, and we encourage you to always set expectations.

Let's recap the five standards for great customer service companies:

1. They know why they are great. In the insurance business, especially in claims, retention tells us whether or not we are doing a great job in customer service.

2. They know where they stand. What is our retention rate?

3. They know where they are going. What is the stated goal in the year ahead for retention?

4. They can accurately describe their jobs. In claims, customer service is what we do. This is all we do.

5. They know what customer service is. For the claims professional, customer service is meeting or exceeding customer's expectations.

Keep your focus on this issue and we promise you, it will make your job easier.

Making the customer feel valued

Jon often shares a story that illustrates the incredible return on investment when we make customers feel like we value them.

AWESOME CLAIMS CUSTOMER SERVICE

Jon's wife was driving her Honda Pilot when she noticed a low tire pressure warning pop up. She was a little nervous about continuing to drive the vehicle, so she called Jon to see what he thought she should do.

Jon, admitting he was no expert, suggested taking the car to the nearest tire store. He looked up the information and directed her to a Discount Tire store in Hudson, Michigan. Jon decided he would help as best he could, he headed to the tire store to make sure there would be no problem, and his wife wasn't talked into some complicated and expensive repair. The store was on the other side of town from where Jon was at the time, so it took him about 30 minutes to get there.

Lots of scenarios were running through his brain:

1. The tire had to be replaced along with the steel rim and an STP sticker at a total cost of $400.

2. All four tires were replaced with high-grade lifetime steel-belted radial tires hand balanced by a "master tire putter-oner" at a total cost of $2,000.

3. The tire was okay, but they had to replace both front and back suspensions plus a new steering mechanism at a total cost of $6,000.

When Jon finally arrived, he was pleasantly surprised. Discount Tire had already pulled off the tire, patched it, and put it back on the vehicle. A much better scenario than Jon could have imagined. No sales pitch, no up selling, no 5-year program to sign up for, nothing. Just fast service of what needed to be done and nothing more.

Nevertheless, there was still the matter of paying for this prompt service. What would this be? $100? $200? $300? Jon was already working on his negotiation technique to prepare for when the big fat number came up. Jon walked up to the service manager and asked for the damage (with a look of shock well-rehearsed). Jon was amazed when the manager said, "There is no charge. We are happy to patch up tires as a courtesy for our valuable customers."

Jon had to admit, "But I'm not a customer of yours. We've never been in here before." The manager replied with, "Well maybe that will change. We would love to help you more in the future if we can."

Fast forward 15 years and Jon will tell you not only has he never purchased a set of tires from anywhere else, he has referred friends and family members to that store countless times.

Carl has a similar story. About 16 years ago Carl was moving International Insurance Institute from

AWESOME CLAIMS CUSTOMER SERVICE

Nashville, TN to New Orleans, LA. Carl had been using AlphaGraphics in Brentwood, TN for a number of years for all of the company printing.

Carl called AlphaGraphics and informed them that since there was not an AlphaGraphics in New Orleans, he was going to have to find a printing company in New Orleans to begin using.

About 15 minutes after Carl's call to AlphaGraphics, he got a call from the manager Mark Williams. Mark said, "Carl, you and International Insurance have been such a valuable customer of ours, we really don't want to lose you. Instead of finding a new printing company, how about we keep doing all your printing, and we will ship it to you, free of charge. That way, you won't have the hassle of moving all of your documents to a new printer and getting used to new people. All of us here enjoy working with your team so much, we just hate to lose you."

Under normal circumstances, Carl would not have been persuaded to use an out of town printer but based on Mark doing a very good job of making Carl feel valuable, Carl decided to give it a try. Sure enough, it went quite smoothly to have everything that was printed simply shipped to the office. Actually, it even saved money because in many cases Carl could have items shipped directly to the customer's location, which saved him shipping costs.

International Insurance Institute spends about $100,000 on printing. This includes course catalogs, flyers, brochures, workbooks, conference brochures, etc.

It has now been 16 years since that call from Mark Williams. Think about it, with one phone call, just by making Carl feel valuable, AlphaGraphics held onto $1.6 million in sales.

CHAPTER 4

Responding to the Snide Comment

We said earlier, it would make our job easier if customers would just tell us what they want, or even if they would just listen. As people who monitor phone calls quite a bit, we can tell you that most of the time, it's the claims person who hasn't listened to what the customer said. Sometimes, they are telling us *exactly* what they want. We're just not listening. What we would like you to do is take a look at this role-play and we're going to have a question for you when we're finished with it.

Customer (Mrs. Rose): "Hello?"

AWESOME CLAIMS CUSTOMER SERVICE

Adjuster (Cathy): "Yeah, hi, Mrs. Rose, this is Cathy, from International Insurance. I want to talk to you about your claim."

Customer: "Thanks for calling, *finally!*"

Adjuster: "Yeah, well ahhh... the first thing I want to talk to you about is how to get your car fixed."

So, how did the claims person do? Well, you might think the claims person did just fine. The claims person was being attacked and she took the high road and ignored the snide comment. You heard that snide comment, didn't you? "Thanks for calling, *finally.*" Many of us will do exactly what Cathy did. In order to be polite, we will do the worst thing you can do with a snide comment. We will ignore the person.

Why is this the worst thing you can do with a snide comment? You might think, "Well no, that's the polite thing to do." But think about it. What did this customer just tell us with that snide comment, "Thanks for calling, *finally?*" This customer just said, "My expectations haven't been met and I'm disappointed." In order to be polite, we are ignoring the person. It's the worst thing you can do. Now, you might say no, it's polite to ignore a snide comment. Not to a customer. When the customer has just said, "I'm disappointed at the service I've been getting," that is not a good thing to ignore. Let's say the customer would have said, "You know what, as a good loyal customer who's been paying my premiums on time for the last twelve years, I'm disappointed at the level of service I've received," we wouldn't ignore that would we? Well, that's what this customer just said. This customer just said, "I'm disappointed with the level of service I've received." And our response, often times in claims, in order to be polite, is to ignore the person. It's the worst thing you can do. Why? Because, although not all customers will make snide comments when they are disappointed, when they do, they do so because they're irritated. They do so because they want something. What they want is a reaction. They want some response out of you. They are looking for your reaction. A snide comment over your level of service is not an attack. If you think it's an attack, you are working much too hard. This is not an attack. It's a request. They are requesting your reaction to the fact they are disappointed. They want to know if you care at all.

Of course, we *do* care. Unfortunately, when we ignore that snide comment, we're letting the customer *think* we don't really care. As a matter of fact, we don't even want to discuss it. Now, what happens when you ignore a snide comment? You know what happens. They keep making snide comments, that's right, until they finally do get a reaction out of you. When they make a snide comment,

"Thanks for calling, *finally*," this person is not asking you to admit you're a horrible person. They don't want you to say, "Oh yes, we're scum, and we don't deserve you." This is not what this customer wanted. What did they want? They wanted your reaction. "What is your reaction to the fact that I'm disappointed?" And if we're in the business of providing customer service, we should have a reaction to that statement.

There are four possible responses to a snide comment.

Worst option: *Ignore it*.

The first one, and the worst, is to ignore a snide comment. Why? Because it's a request. And we shouldn't ignore our customer's requests. So, number one, the worst thing you can do, is to ignore the snide comment.

Second worst option: *Blame the customer*.

Number two is to blame the customer. We don't mean to do this at all. We're trying to be polite. But I have heard claims people say things when faced with a comment such as, "Thanks for calling, *finally*," like, "Well, when were you expecting a phone call?" Now the problem with this is there's no end to that conversation that can be anything other than blaming the customer for having a false expectation. "Well, when were you expecting a phone call?" "Oh, I don't know, by two o'clock." "Well, how could we call you by two if you just reported it at one o'clock?" There isn't an end to the conversation that's going to end up any other way than the customer feeling blamed for having a false expectation. We're blaming the customer for being unreasonable for having a false expectation. That's all fine and good except for one thing: Somebody could have set that customer's expectation. Imagine, in this case, Cathy was making her first contact with this customer and that customer had already called in and they were told Cathy would be calling today. Now Cathy is calling and, of course, the customer is irritated because in her mind, this has taken too long. What if, when we had that customer on the phone, they would have been told, "You know what, Cathy will be calling you by five o'clock today." Now maybe when Cathy calls at four o'clock, the customer isn't irritated. You see, we had the opportunity to set the customer's expectation and we didn't take it. To blame a customer for having a false expectation anytime in the claims process when we have most of the control isn't fair. So, the second worst thing you can do is to blame the customer.

AWESOME CLAIMS CUSTOMER SERVICE

Third worst option: Explain it.

The third worst thing you can do with a snide comment is to explain it. Even if nothing went wrong, in the customer's mind something did go wrong so what does offering them explanations when they are irritated sound like? Excuses? Right. And do excuses ever calm customers down? No, they almost always make them irritated. Allow us to share with you a real live story. Carl was monitoring a phone call at one particular company and heard the customer make a comment that the company didn't have a very good phone system. The customer said, "You know, I'm always getting transferred around with you guys. It's pretty frustrating." The claims person goes through the explanation mode, saying, "Well, we just got this new phone system and we're trying to get a handle on it, and this other department is in a meeting, so we're trying to take their calls" and goes on and on and on with the customer. Do you think that solved the customer's issue? Do you think that calmed the customer down? Do you think that customer said, "Oh really, now I understand. Oh, I feel so foolish. Let me withdraw my comment." No, it didn't calm the customer down. She just got more angry and said, "Well why don't you guys get a better phone system then!" and the claims person said, "Well, we were going to but we lost money in the budget and duh de duh duh..." Now they went back and forth and they're talking about phone money budget!

Carl couldn't believe his ears. This actually happened. Later in the afternoon, another caller called in with a very different result.

In this case, a different claims person got a phone call with almost the exact same issue. "I'm always getting transferred around with you people. It's pretty frustrating." In this case, the claims person said, "You know what, if you've been transferred around, I know that's no fun. I'm sorry this happened to you. Now that you've reached me, how can I help you?" Now let us ask you a question: Who do you think had an easier time with the customer? The first claims person, who gave a bunch of excuses, or the second claims person, who simply said, "I'm sorry this happened to you." Think about it. When people make snide comments, what are they looking for? They're not looking for you to admit you're a horrible person. They're asking you, "What is your reaction to the fact that I'm disappointed?" And our reaction should be, "I'm sorry."

Fourth and best option: Simply apologize.

Your fourth option to a snide comment is to simply apologize. Apologize in a general sense. Notice the claims person said, "If you've been transferred around, I'm sorry." The claims person didn't say, "I'm sorry for transferring you around," he simply said, "If you have been transferred around, I'm sorry about that." That's what this person was looking for.

Let's go back and give Cathy another chance at this. Tell us how you think she does.

Customer (Mrs. Rose): "Hello?"

Adjuster (Cathy): "Yeah, hi Mrs. Rose. This is Cathy, from International Insurance. I'm calling about your claim."

Customer: "Thanks for calling, *finally!*"

Adjuster: "Oh, Mrs. Rose, I apologize if it took a little longer than you were thinking. I just want to talk to you about getting your car fixed."

Customer: "OK, what's going on?"

Well, how did Cathy do the second time? We think she did better. Notice she just apologized for the fact the customer is disappointed and was ready to move on. Now, let us ask you this: Is this going to turn the customer into Little Ms. Sunshine? Is she going to say, "Oh boy, am I glad I had a claim now!" No, she might even still be irritated. But you know what, she won't be irritated with Cathy. And she's the one whose job just got easier today, because she paid attention to what the customer was actually asking for. We said it would make our job easier if customers would tell us what they want. When customers make a snide comment, they're telling us exactly what they want. They want our reaction. So, would it be so terrible if we told them we're sorry they are disappointed? These are our customers. We're in the customer service business. This is what we do for a living. It wouldn't be so bad if we let a customer know we're sorry they're disappointed. Let us ask you this: If we were to say to a customer, "You know what, I'm sorry you're disappointed," would our kidneys just shut down? Would our lungs just collapse on us? Would we be able to survive it? A funny thing about it is in claims, and we were both claims adjusters and claims supervisors and managers, so we understand this, in claims, sometimes we get attacked so much that apologizing is the last thing that comes across our mind. But in this case what we have to recognize is this person is not attacking us. They are asking us for something. "What is your reaction to the fact that I am disappointed?"

Something else we hear quite a bit is people who say, "Well, when you apologize to people, you lose credibility, don't you think?" Well, let us answer that. We don't think so. We are in the business of providing customer service and sometimes people are telling us exactly what they want. You know what most people, when they make snide comments, get? You know what they're used to getting? They're used to getting ignored. They're used to getting blamed. They're used to getting a bunch of stupid excuses. You know what they are not used to? Somebody saying, I'm sorry. You deserve better than that as my customer. They're not used to this. You're going to gain tremendous credibility in this person's eyes. And we said before that gaining a customer's trust would make our job easier.

We are big fans of practice so we're going to give you the chance to do that right now. One of our favorite sayings is *as you practice, so shall you do.* Here's what we'd like you to imagine. You return to your desk (maybe you were at lunch) and there's a message on your desk that says you need to call Mrs. Smith. You go ahead and call Mrs. Smith and say, "Yes, I'm calling you back" and she says, "Oh, so people at your company really *do* return phone calls, huh..." Before you might have ignored a snide comment in order to be polite. But now you know differently. What we would like you to do is take a moment and write down what you think the proper response would be given with what we've just talked about. OK, her comment is, "Oh, so people at your company do return phone calls, huh..." What would you say in response?

Well, given your newfound training, we're sure you came up with something pretty good. Before we give you our response, we want to tell you about a true story. Carl was monitoring a phone call when he actually heard this. Somebody had called up a customer, returning a phone call and the customer made that exact comment, "Oh, so people at your company do return phone calls, huh..." The claims person's response was, "Well, yeah, we return phone calls. Why, you didn't get a return phone call before?" and she said, "No, I haven't." He then said, "Well, maybe your answering machine wasn't working" and they got into an argument back and forth. Carl went out to that claims person and said, "Why did you take offense at this?" And he said, "Well, she said I don't return my phone calls." So, Carl pointed out, "Well, she wasn't even talking about you. Obviously, you are returning your phone calls. Clearly, she must be talking about somebody else. Why are you taking this personally? You don't need to."

Our response would be, "You know what, if you haven't gotten a return phone call in the past, I am sorry about that. We do recognize returning phone calls is important. I'm sorry that didn't happen. I always return my phone calls. How can I help you?" Say something nice and sweet. Sorry it didn't happen in the past, let's move on. Remember, when people make snide comments, they don't want to attack you. They don't want you to admit you're a horrible person. They don't even want to find out the issue. They don't want to get down to the bottom of things. You know what they want? They want your reaction, and your reaction should be, "I'm sorry about that." Now you have a chance to take a look at another scenario. Cathy is going to try this again. Tell us how you think she does.

Customer (Mrs. Rose): "Hello?"

Adjuster (Cathy): "Ah...yes Mrs. Rose, this is Cathy with International Insurance Institute. I'm calling to take a recorded statement from you regarding your claim."

Customer: "Wow, it's amazing how quick you call me when you need something."

Adjuster: "Yeah, I want to talk to you about your claim."

How did she do? Well, not too good given our training, right? In this case, when a customer says, "Oh, you only call when you need something," our reaction might be, "You know what, if it seems like we only call when we need something, I am sorry about that. We do want to be responsive to your needs. Let me explain why I'm calling and then see if there's something I can do to help you."

Let's recap the four possible responses to a snide comment:

1. We can ignore it. But you know what, we're in the customer service business and when a customer tells us they want something, we shouldn't ignore it.

2. We can blame the customer. We can blame the customer for having a false expectation, but you know what, we set expectations. So that's not fair.

3. We can explain it. That's all fine and good except explanations sound a lot like excuses and we're not here to give excuses.

4. We can simply apologize. Apologize for the fact that they are disappointed.

Remember, we said that it would make our job easier if customers would just tell us what they want. A person who makes a snide comment is telling us exactly what they want: They want your reaction to the fact that they're disappointed. Do you care at all? One of these four responses will make your job much, much, easier.

Sometimes you may need to offer a general apology for a customer service interaction that might not have gone well. Do not miss this opportunity to make things right. If you miss the opportunity, it will slow the process and prevent you from following the strategy you have learned. Be sure to offer the apology and then refocus the customer on the process at hand.

CHAPTER 5

Gaining Cooperation

Now you know how to deal with the snide comment and that's a good skill. We talked before about getting customers to cooperate thereby making our jobs easier. Not ignoring a snide comment won't do that; that's just getting a landmine out of the way. What we need to learn is how to gain cooperation.

We've heard good, hard working, well intentioned claims people often using the wrong words and the wrong terms and basically the wrong approach when trying to gain cooperation. Many times, in claims, to a customer, it almost sounds like we are daring them not to cooperate. I dare you: Don't sign that medical authorization form. I dare you: Don't release your car. I dare you: Don't send in those receipts. I double dog dare you. We don't mean to do this but often, the way we ask customers to do something often sounds like a threat or an ultimatum. It's a big challenge to overcome this but we are going to do it. We're going to teach you a three-step process that should be invaluable to you when you are trying to gain cooperation from a customer.

Here is an important point before we get started. What many claims people don't appreciate is that when you ask a customer to cooperate, you've really begun a negotiation process. If you tell them they need to do something and they say OK, the negotiation is over. But if they say no, you're actually in the negotiation process. Do you know that as a claims professional, you only spend ten percent of your time negotiating the dollar amount of something? Only ten percent. The other ninety percent of the time you spend negotiating, you're negotiating for something else. What would that be? Cooperation. Believe it or not, just getting people to do something, return your phone calls, meet you out at a loss, mail in an estimate, sign a form, any time you ask a customer to do something, you're asking them to cooperate. You're actually in a negotiation process. You will spend much more time negotiating for cooperation than you will spend negotiating the dollar amount of something. That's what's important to understand as we start this process.

Let us look at a new role-play. In this case, a claims professional is calling up a customer to ask her to sign a medical authorization form.

Customer (Mrs. Rose): "Hello?"

Adjuster (Cathy): "Yes, Mrs. Rose, this is Cathy from International Insurance. I'm calling in regard to those medical authorizations I sent you a while back. I still haven't received them."

Customer: "Yes, Cathy, I've got those papers but I'm not going to sign them."

Adjuster: "Oh, umm Mrs. Rose, you realize that if you don't sign and return those medical authorizations, there's actually going to be no way we can pay your medical bills."

Customer: "Cathy, I'm not going to sign those papers, and you will pay me."

Adjuster: "Ahh...Mrs. Rose, you realize it's your obligation under the policy to cooperate and by not signing those, you're actually in violation of your policy and there could be no coverage at all for you."

Customer: "Well I'm telling you right now, I'm not signing them."

AWESOME CLAIMS CUSTOMER SERVICE

Adjuster: "Mrs. Rose, we need you to sign those medical authorizations."

Customer: "Not going to happen."

Well, how did he do? Did that look a little familiar? Well, we have all seen it. Cathy pulled out the claims hammer. You know what that is. If you don't cooperate, we can show you how we can hurt you. Bam! If you don't sign this form, we can't pay you. Bam! We keep whacking on people sometimes until they finally give in. So, it's called the claims hammer, which is all fine and good. It does work. It gets people to move. But remember, we're in the customer service business. This person has already had something bad happen to them. They don't need any more pain and anguish. It's a good tool but there's an old saying, *when all you have is a hammer, everything looks like a nail*. You know what that means. It doesn't matter if you need sandpaper. It doesn't matter if you need a pair of pliers. It doesn't matter if you need a saw. If all you have is a hammer, you're going to use it—even if it's the wrong tool. Why? Because it's all you've got, and what do you do with a hammer? You hit things with it. We have a nice, big, fat, hammer in claims we like to pull out all of the time. It does get people to move but we have to have a different approach.

What we want to teach you is a three-step process that you can use to gain cooperation without all the pain and the bloodshed. In order to help you understand the first step, we'd like to tell you a little story.

We're going to tell you the story and we want you to tell us what you think the first step in negotiating for cooperation should be. It should be obvious to you. This particular story is told in the book *The 8 Characteristics of the Awesome Adjuster*. We get asked all the time if this is a true story. Yeah, it's true. Here's what happened.

This particular claims adjuster is calling up a customer to settle a total loss car. He has a fair market evaluation that says the car is worth $2,500. So, he calls up the customer and says, "We want to pay you $2,500 for your car." The customer says, "No way, I feel my car is worth $3,000." The adjuster pulls out the claims hammer. "Well, we have a report here that says it's worth $2,500." Bam! It doesn't work. The customer says, "Well, I don't care what that says. I feel my car is worth $3,000." Since that doesn't work the adjuster figures he'll torture him a little bit. "Well, sir, if you don't take the $2,500, we can't pay your storage fees." Jab! How do you like that? Ouch! Well, now the guy is bleeding all over the place. The guy says, "I don't care. I still feel my car is worth $3,000." The adjuster says, "Well, then we can't pay your rental anymore either." Jab! How do you like that? Ouch! Now the guy is bleeding out of both sides. The adjuster figures he's bound to give in pretty soon, right? So, then the customer says, "I don't care what you say, I'm not going to take $2,500." Finally, the adjuster says, "Well, sir, you don't have to take the $2,500 but you're the one who's still going to have to make car payments." Squash! So now we have hit him on the head with a hammer. We've tortured him a little bit and we've stomped on him, and of course, the claim remains unsettled.

This doesn't happen very often, but Carl went out to the claims adjuster and said, "You know, I think if you would have changed your process, just slightly, you could have gotten this guy to agree with you. You gave him no reason to agree with you. All you did was give him information so he would give in. It's much easier to convince someone you're right than it is to get them to give in if they think you're wrong. That takes a lot of pain and a lot of hitting, as you just saw. Why didn't you try to convince him you're right? It would have been easier." You know what this adjuster said to Carl? He said, "He'll get tired of walking." You know what? That adjuster isn't wrong. He's right. In a week from now, this customer is going to call up and say, "OK fine, I'll take your $2,500, you stupid thieves." So, this claim will get settled but what will happen in the meantime? This customer will call and complain and tell every single person he knows what terrible service he's gotten. This outcome is avoidable.

So, let us ask you this: What question did the claims person never ask the customer? Why? Why do you feel your car is worth $3,000? He never even asked one time. Why? To him, why didn't matter. He had his facts, and he was going to hit the customer with the facts.

Carl did something he almost never does. He called this customer, and said, "Yes, my name is Carl Van. I was monitoring your call for quality assurance." Of course, the customer complained for a little while. "You guys are really terrible." "I know but let me ask you a couple of questions." Carl asked him a couple of questions then finally said, "By the way, I'm kind of curious, why do you feel your car is worth $3,000?" The answer to that question had nothing to do with car payments. It had nothing to do with storage charges. It had nothing to do with rental fees. It had nothing to do with what this adjuster was literally beating him to death with. The adjuster just didn't know because he never asked why. This customer said, "Look, my brother gave me this car, and I know you don't care about that. You're going to tell me it doesn't matter but, you know what, it's important to me because he died about six months ago and he gave me this car and it means a lot to me. Somebody had offered him $3,000 for this car, and I'm not going to let you guys rip him off." Notice what he said. He didn't say rip *me* off. He said rip *him* off. This customer is convinced that if he takes a penny less than $3,000, he's letting an insurance company rip off his dead brother. Now, do you think he's going to be swayed by storage charges? Do you think rental fees are going to mean a whole lot to this person? None of that is going to mean anything to him. The adjuster just didn't know it because he never asked...why.

Step One: Ask why.

The first step in gaining cooperation when you ask somebody to do something is to ask them why they won't do it. Why would you ask that? Because most of the time, people's reasons for cooperating have nothing to do with the issue at hand. It's just their reasons, and those reasons are unrelated to the facts. One of the maxims we teach in our negotiation classes is *great negotiators never argue reasons; they argue the facts.* What they do is find out the reasons and get them out of the way, which is what we would like to show you.

Here is another role-play. In this case, the adjuster does the right thing. She does ask, why. See what happens after that.

Customer (Mrs. Rose): "Hello."

Adjuster (Cathy): "Ah, yes, Mrs. Rose, this is Cathy from International Insurance. I'm calling to follow up on those medical authorizations we sent you a while back. We still haven't received those yet."

Customer: "Cathy, I'm not going to sign those papers."

Adjuster: "Is it OK if I ask you why?"

Customer: "Well, my neighbor is in his second year of law school and he told me not to sign anything."

Adjuster: "Yeah but with all due respect Mrs. Rose, what does he really know about claims?"

Cathy certainly did better that time, didn't she? She did ask why and now she knows why. Unfortunately, she doesn't have the second step. She's not a bad person, she just hasn't been trained, which is what we want to do now. In this case, once she finds out why, she doesn't know to do anything other than argue. And in claims, that's a pretty big tool for us. We've had claims people tell us, "You know for 15 years; I didn't know to do anything other than argue with people." We honestly believe that the only way to convince someone we're right is to show that they're wrong. But remember what we said before: *Great negotiators never argue reasons; they argue the facts.* You know what they do with someone's reasons? They do the exact opposite. They acknowledge them.

Step Two: Acknowledge.

Step number two is to acknowledge. Acknowledgment is a very powerful tool in claims. We said before that it would make our jobs so much easier if people were just reasonable. And we mentioned earlier on, sometimes we say things that make people unreasonable. One of the worst things you could tell somebody if you want them to be reasonable is, "You are going to have to be reasonable." When you say that, you have just called them an unreasonable person. And now, if the person changes their mind, they have proven that they have been unreasonable. What are you going to get most of the time when you tell people, "You're going to have to be reasonable?" You are going to get the person to say, "I *am* being reasonable." Now you actually have the customer admitting that, if they change their mind, which is what you wanted, they've been unreasonable. It's one of the worst things you can say. If you want someone to be reasonable, you say something very different. If you want someone to be reasonable, you demonstrate that you already think they *are* being reasonable by acknowledging their point of view. As a matter of fact, another maxim that we have in customer service and negotiations is this: People will consider what you have to say to the exact degree that you demonstrate you understand their point of view. We are going to repeat that because it's so important. People will consider what you have to say to the exact degree that you demonstrate you understand their point of view.

From your gut, isn't it easier to talk to someone when they demonstrate they understand your point of view? Just inherently, does it feel right to you that people will probably pay more attention to you when you've shown them that you understand them rather than when you are trying to prove them wrong? What's the number one way to prove someone wrong? Argue with them. That's what you're doing when you're arguing with someone. You are trying to show that they are wrong. What did we say great negotiators never do? They never argue with reasons. One of the concepts that we need to embrace is that people can't be wrong for their reasons because most of the time, their reasons have nothing to do with the facts at hand. Anything the person tells us as to why they're not cooperating usually has nothing to do with the facts at hand. It doesn't matter what someone's neighbor said. All that matters is that we need the forms signed in order to get these bills paid. Notice the reasons have nothing to do with the facts at hand. We want to acknowledge their point of view to demonstrate we understand it and show them we already think they're being reasonable. Once someone believes we think they are being reasonable, they can change their mind and still be a reasonable person. This is key for us.

Step Three: Get back to the facts.

What we want to do is get back to the facts.

The three steps for gaining cooperation:

1. Ask the customer why they won't cooperate.

2. Acknowledge their point of view as reasonable. Not that you agree with them. Not that they're right. Just that you understand and appreciate their point of view.

3. Get back to the facts. Talk to them about why we need to do what we need to do in order to help them. The facts are we need these forms signed so we can get your bills paid. Acknowledge their point of view but get back to the facts.

Let us give Cathy one more opportunity.

Customer (Mrs. Rose): "Hello."

Adjuster (Cathy): "Yes, hello Mrs. Rose, this is Cathy with International Insurance. I'm calling to follow up on the medical authorizations we sent you a while back. We still haven't received those yet."

Customer: "Cathy, I'm not going to sign those papers."

Adjuster: "Ah... can I ask you why not?"

Customer: "Well, my neighbor is in his second year of law school and he informed me that I should not sign any papers."

Adjuster: "You know, I can perfectly understand that Mrs. Rose. If you've bounced this off somebody you trust, that's perfectly reasonable. By signing the authorization, it will allow us to get those medical bills for you and we can get those medical bills that much sooner. If you would like to run this by your neighbor, I'd be more than happy to help you with that."

Customer: "Fine."

Cathy did much better, don't you agree? Notice what she did. She focused on acknowledging their reasons then got back to the facts. Great negotiators never argue reasons; they argue the facts. If we want to make our jobs easier and make customers want to cooperate and get them to be reasonable, we have to demonstrate that we think they already are being reasonable. Then they can change their mind. What we want to do now is show you another scenario, different reason this time, and what we're going to want you to do, ultimately, but not just yet, is to decide what you think the right answer would be. For now, look at this scenario.

Adjuster (Dave): "Hello, claims, this is Dave Vanderpan, can I help you?"

Customer (Laura Wimsatt): "Hi, this is Laura Wimsatt and my mother told me I needed to give you guys a call."

Adjuster: "Yes, Ms. Wimsatt, thank you for calling back. I was calling in regard to some forms we sent you a few days back. We need you to fill those out, sign them, and then send those back to me as soon as possible."

Customer: "Well, I'm not signing anything."

Adjuster: "Well, can I ask you why not?"

Customer: "Well, when I reported this, someone at your company told me that I wouldn't have to sign anything."

Adjuster: "Alright, well, who told you that?"

Customer: "Well, I don't know, someone from your company."

Adjuster: "Well, Ms. Wimsatt, you're dealing with me now, so I really do need you to sign those, and send them back to me as soon as possible. Can you do that for me?"

Not as good that time. Dave did use the first step. He did ask why. What happened when he got the information? He slipped right back into the argument mode. And by the way, if you start to ask things like, "Well, who told you that?" what you're really saying to the customer is, "Well, either you're lying or you're stupid, let's go find out which," right? Notice we don't have to argue with people's reasons. Sometimes in claims, it's just burned into us that the only way we can convince people that we're right is to show them they're wrong. We now know that's not true. If you want someone to believe you're right, focus on the fact you're right, acknowledge their point of view, and get back to the facts.

Dave did the first step but fell a little short on the second step. Here is what we would like you to do. We would like you to come up with what you think the right response would be. In this case, you've just asked the customer to sign a medical authorization form. They said no. You asked why and they gave you that exact answer: "I was told by someone at your company that I wouldn't have to sign anything." What would be the proper acknowledgment phrase? Take a moment and write down your answer.

We are sure you came up with a very good response and there are plenty of very good responses to that particular scenario. Here's our suggestion. You ask a customer to sign a medical form and they say, no. Ask them why not and they tell you, "Well, because I was told I wouldn't have to sign anything." Rather than argue with them, a better response would probably be, "You know what, if you were told you wouldn't have to sign anything, I can certainly understand why you wouldn't want to. That's what you were told. That's reasonable. I appreciate that. I do apologize for the fact that someone gave you the wrong information. This form allows us to get your medical bills so we can pay you. If you would be willing to sign this form and get this to me, I can make sure your bills get paid. But I am sorry that someone gave you the wrong information." Maybe something along those lines is what we are looking for. The point is, the more time you spend acknowledging someone's point of view, the more likely they will listen to what you have to say. People will consider your point of view to the exact degree you demonstrate you understand their point of view.

The best way to communicate that you understand someone's point of view is to repeat what they said back to them, to acknowledge it. By the way, saying, "Well, yes but..." will not work. "Well, I understand but..." tells the customer you don't understand. So, if they say, "I'm not going to sign that form because, I was told I wouldn't have to sign anything." You would have to say, "You know what, if you were told you wouldn't have to sign anything, I can understand why you wouldn't want to. That's reasonable." "Yes but..." will not work so don't think it will. You have to take the time to repeat what was said. *The more you convince someone you understand their point of view, the more they will consider your point of view.*

This powerful tool can also let you know when your understanding is incorrect. Let's assume you can't repeat back what the customer said to you. "Well, you don't want to sign this form because...because... Why don't you want to sign this form again?" This might happen to you. Don't be surprised if it does. If you can't repeat something back to someone, guess what it tells you? You don't understand their point of view. You are not going to be able to acknowledge it. Don't be surprised if you end up in an argument. It also indicates you probably weren't listening. What did we say before? We have to do a good job of listening to customers if we want them to listen to us. The acknowledgement piece is a very, very, powerful tool.

The other issue is it will help gain customer trust, and having customers trust us makes our jobs easier. Let's talk about this idea for a second. Remember we talked about the claims hammer? It's our tool. It lets people know we can hurt them. As a claims person, threatening someone is the easiest way to make them not trust you. Give somebody an ultimatum and they will never trust you again. It's going to be why they argue with everything you say. It's going to be why they challenge everything you do.

The number one thing you can do to get people to trust you is to use the word *help*. People like to be helped, and they don't like to be threatened. Customers trust people who are trying to help them, and they don't trust people who are trying to threaten them or give them ultimatums. Use the word *help* quite a bit. So even in the scenario of trying to get people to be reasonable and cooperate, you can use this tool quite a bit. You could say things like, "If you don't want to sign this form because you were told you wouldn't have to; I can certainly appreciate that. That does make sense. My goal is to make sure that I *help* you get your bills paid. This form allows me to do that. Let me *help* you by signing this form." So you see, the more you use the word *help*, believe it or not, the more people might trust you—especially if you are taking the time to acknowledge their point of view while you are doing it.

Here's a great example. It's one of our favorites. We actually hear this quite a bit. In this scenario, we are going to try to get a customer to cooperate. Follow what happens and see if you can catch what upset this customer so much.

Customer (Mrs. Rose): "Hello?"

Adjuster (Cathy): "Yes, hello, Mrs. Rose, this is Cathy with International Insurance. I'm calling to follow up on those medical authorizations I sent you a while back. I still haven't received them."

Customer: "Right. I'm not signing those papers."

Adjuster: "Well, Mrs. Rose, is there any particular reason why you won't sign them?"

Customer: "There's a *damn* good reason why I'm not signing those papers!"

In claims, we will say to someone, "Well, is there any reason why you won't sign this form? Is there any reason why you won't do this?" Think about what we're asking. We are actually implying the customer does things for no reason. "Do you have a reason for the things you do? Or are you one of those babbling idiots I deal with?" We don't mean to say that, but the question implies the customer may be a person who does things for no reason. Of course, there's a reason. By asking if there is a reason, believe it or not, some people are going to become upset. So, why bother using that phrase? Instead, you want to ask them *what* the reason is. "*Why* won't you cooperate?" That's the key. Don't upset people just by the way you ask them for information. That's a dangerous thing to do.

AWESOME CLAIMS CUSTOMER SERVICE

We want to avoid arguing with customers, as we talked about. There's one concept that's very important and we want to hit on it: When two people are in an argument, most psychologists will tell you that people want to be understood more than any other aspect of the argument. People want to be understood even more than whatever it is they are arguing about. We have a very powerful, inherent need as human beings to want to be understood. So, what we don't want to do is violate this concept in our process of dealing with our customers. Make sure that you take enough time to acknowledge someone's point of view so you can move on to the facts.

Consider the following scenario. Let's say you have a customer and you're trying to take a recorded statement, something that we all do, worker's comp, property, auto, everybody takes recorded statements. In this case, you might be a worker's comp person and you're calling up a customer to take a recorded statement. So, you call them up and you say, "Hey, I would like to take your recorded statement" and they say, no. Well, you now know you're going to ask, "Can you tell me why you wouldn't want to give a recorded statement?" and they say, "Yeah, because you'll just use it against me." That's their reason. With your newfound skill, we would like to have you write out what you think the proper response would be. How would you acknowledge that person's point of view? We want you to write down word for word what you would say to incorporate what they said to you as part of your response. Take a moment and write down your response.

Did you come up with a good answer? You know, if somebody said to one of us, "I'm not going to give you a recorded statement" and when we asked why not, they replied, "Because you'll just use it against me," the best response would probably be, "You know what, if you don't want to give me a recorded statement because you're concerned I'm going to use it against you, I can understand that. I appreciate that. I'll tell you what. I don't want to use this against you. What I want to do is get down to the bottom of things and you know what, there are always two sides to every story, and you're entitled to have your say. What I would like to do is take your statement so we can consider your point of view because you are entitled to that. Would you do that for me?" Now maybe this person will say yes or maybe they'll say, no. But you know what, they are much more likely to agree than if we start to argue with them. We like to use this scenario because Carl heard this when he was monitoring. A claims adjuster asked a customer, "Can I take your recorded statement?" and the customer said, no. The adjuster asked why not, and the customer replied, "Because you'll just use it against me." And you know what the adjuster said? "Well why would I use it against you?" And immediately, what did the adjuster start doing? Arguing with their reasons. You don't have to argue with reasons. You have got to move on to the facts. Pay attention to the way you do that.

AWESOME CLAIMS CUSTOMER SERVICE

Recapping the three steps for gaining cooperation:

1. Ask why. Find out from the customer why they are not cooperating.

2. Acknowledge their point of view. You don't have to agree with them or tell them they're right, but you do have to let them know you appreciate their point of view. Be sure to repeat it back to them to prove you understand.

3. Get back to talking about the facts. If you can use the word *help* while you are giving them the facts, all the better. But make sure you are talking about the facts of what it is you need to do and not spending time arguing with them.

Adjuster (Dave): "Yes, hello, is Laura Wimsatt there please?"

Customer (Ms. Wimsatt): "This is she."

Adjuster: "Yeah, hi, Ms. Wimsatt, this is Dave Vanderpan with International Insurance. I'm calling about the medical authorizations we sent you a few days ago. We need you to sign those and make sure you send those back to us right away."

Customer: "Umm... I don't really want to sign any forms."

Adjuster: "Can I ask you why not?"

Customer: "Well, I had an embarrassing surgery a couple of years ago and I'm not really comfortable with that information being out about me."

Adjuster: "I can completely understand that. If you had an embarrassing operation and you don't want people to see that, I can understand. Our goal here isn't to embarrass you, it's actually to help you, Ms. Wimsatt, and by signing that authorization, we'll ensure that we get those medical bills as quickly as possible. We will do everything we can to not get the ones that are sensitive that you mentioned. If by chance we do happen to receive those, we'll handle those as professionally as we possibly can. So, if you could, please sign and send that in. Can you do that for us?"

Customer: "Alright, I guess that's fine."

Adjuster: "Well, thank you."

Dave did a great job there didn't he? He asked why, acknowledged the customer's point of view, and got back to the facts. Why do we take such care? Because we're in the customer service business, and in this particular case, this customer let us know, "You know what, I don't want to be embarrassed." So, rather than argue with the customer, maybe what we should communicate is we don't want to embarrass you, we want to help you.

Carl was teaching a class in Cincinnati one time and got a call from a friend, "Carl, I'm teaching a class in Cincinnati near you. I can't find a room anywhere. I've got to get on the plane. Can you help me find a room?" "Sure, I'll go ahead and give it a try." Carl said. So, Carl called the 800 number from the phone at the hotel. "I've got a friend coming in tonight, and he needs a room." They said, "No problem, we're not even a third booked. He doesn't even need to make a reservation, just bring him in." Great, no problem...

Carl went and picked up his friend at the airport and brought him back to the hotel. Carl walked up to the front desk and said, "I got my friend here. He needs a room for the night." The desk clerk looked it up and said, "Oh, we're completely booked." Carl said, "Wait a minute. You don't understand. I was told there were plenty of rooms. I even called the 800 number." The clerk looked it up again and said, "There are no rooms here. There's nothing I can do sir." Carl said, "You don't understand, this makes me feel like an idiot. This puts me in a very bad position. I told my friend there would be a room and now you are saying there aren't any." Carl starts to get a little angry. You know what that clerk does? He takes the terminal and turns it around towards Carl like he must be stupid. "Sir, we have no rooms, look."

Let us ask you a question: Do you think he gained credibility with his actions? He was throwing a lot of facts at Carl. He was trying to prove Carl wrong, but do you think he gained a lot of credibility with him? No, he didn't gain any credibility. As a matter of fact, Carl said, "You know what? I want to talk to a manager right now. Go get me a manager." So, the desk clerk walks over, talks to this woman, and says, "Hey Judy, this guy wants to talk to you." We all know what *this guy* means, right? So, Judy walks over and says, "Sir, how can I help you?" Carl told her the whole story. "Oh... my friend called, and I called the 800 number and now I bring him in and there's no room." Carl goes through the whole story. You know what she does? She looks it up on her terminal and says, "You know what Mr. Van; I am so sorry. I can see the situation you're in, and I can certainly appreciate your point of view. You know what, whoever you were talking to at the 800 number must have been looking at the wrong screen because we have been booked for over a week. I'm so sorry. I do appreciate your point of view and you know what, if there was a room here tonight that I could give you, I would give it to you because I do appreciate the situation you're in. The truth is we really just don't have a room. Can I help you find a room somewhere else?" In this case, two people told Carl no.

AWESOME CLAIMS CUSTOMER SERVICE

Who is more credible: the first person or the second person? Is it the person who said "No" and threw a lot of facts at Carl or the person who said, "I understand your point of view and the situation you're in?"

We deny claims all the time and we say things like, "Well, you're not entitled to it" or "We won't pay it." To tell a customer we're not going to pay them is OK, but would it kill us to say, "You know what, I'd really love to be able to pay that, but the policy doesn't allow it. I'd love to do it if I could, but I can't." To tell people we want to be able to help them is a very powerful thing. In this case, the manager of this hotel did nothing more than acknowledge Carl's situation thereby automatically gaining more credibility with Carl than the desk clerk.

We are firm believers in the three steps to gaining cooperation. We have seen it used by claims people not only to gain cooperation but to gain trust from the customer. They identify what's important to the customer, communicate an understanding of the customer's situation, and get back to the facts.

Some of you might go to swap meets. Sometimes we call them flea markets. Carl likes to go because he can negotiate with the people selling their stuff. Carl was at one flea market, and there was someone selling stereos. Carl was off at another booth when a customer approached the stereo booth. However, Carl was able to hear their entire conversation.

"Hey, how much for that stereo?"

"300 bucks."

"300 bucks? It's not worth 300 bucks."

"Yes, it is."

"Well, look it's got a little scratch on it right here."

This customer was doing what we all tend to do. We tend to argue in order to convince someone we're right. Well, of course the seller felt insulted, and he said, "No, it's worth $300. It's just a tiny little scratch. Who cares? I paid $600 for this thing six months ago." Can you just hear this conversation? So, the customer says, "Well, it's probably obsolete then right?" "No, it's not obsolete, it's perfectly good" and they're going back and forth and back and forth, and finally, the customer says, "I wouldn't give you 200 bucks for it." The seller replies, "I wouldn't take 200 bucks from you." "Fine!" and the customer walks off.

Carl knew this customer took the wrong approach, so he decided he was going to try something. Carl turned to his wife who was nearby, and he said, "Hey honey, watch this." "No, Carl, don't. We have enough stereos." Nevertheless, he decided to give his skills a try. Carl went up to the person selling stereos.

"So, how much for that stereo?"

"300 bucks" (with a grumpy attitude— he's still mad from the last guy)

"300 bucks—Well, that's great. I mean this is a great stereo. It's only got little scratch on it."

"Yeah, that last guy said it wasn't worth 200 bucks."

"Well, he's crazy. Obviously, it's worth $300. I mean, you must have paid $500 or $600 for this thing, didn't you?"

"Yeah, I did. I paid 600 bucks just a few months ago."

"Well that's great. 300 bucks, there's no doubt this thing is worth 300 bucks, no doubt at all. I only brought $200 with me though. I'm sorry."

Carl started to walk away, and right then he says, "How about $250?" So, let us ask you a question: Why did he drop his price for Carl immediately, yet he wouldn't budge for the other guy? Because Carl didn't care what it was worth. He's selling it for $300. That's what it's worth. He has his reasons. What does Carl care? Guess what Carl cares about? What he's going to pay for it. You want it to be worth $300, fine. Heck, it's worth $400. What does Carl care? You have your reasons but now let's get back to the facts. Great negotiators never argue with reasons. They argue the facts. Stick to this concept and you're going to find your job getting much easier. We promise you.

CHAPTER 6

The Empathic Connection

For this next part, we want to introduce a new concept called *the empathic connection*. In order to do that though, we want to use a real-life scenario Carl heard when he was monitoring phone calls. In this case, a claims adjuster was trying to get a customer to go out and get an estimate. Now this was a claimant, our insured had run into this person and the adjuster was calling up just to say, "Would you please go get an estimate and send it in so I can pay it?" It was minor damage. The car was perfectly drivable. "Would you please go do that?" Now in this case, the person lived way off in the middle of nowhere, there were no independent adjusters that could do the work, they were off on some CAT duty and there were no drive-ins. So really, the only option for this adjuster was to ask the customer to send in an estimate. For this scenario, we will use Doug Baker, who is our project manager, and who will be the claims adjuster, asking the customer to send in the estimate. Carl will be the customer this time. Alright, so let's get started.

Customer (Carl Van): "Hello, Carl Van."

Adjuster (Doug Baker): "This is Doug, with ABC Insurance. I'm calling about your claim."

Customer: "Uh huh, what's up?"

Adjuster: "I need you to send in an estimate on your car."

Customer: "You want me to send in an estimate?"

Adjuster: "Yes, I do."

Customer: "So I've got to go out and get one and send it to you?"

Adjuster: "Absolutely."

Customer: "No way man, no way!"

Adjuster: "Well, can I ask you why?"

Customer: "Yeah, you can ask why. Because you guys ran into me. I'm the victim here. I'm the victim, why should I run around doing your job?"

Adjuster: "Ahh...well..."

We struggle normally in this situation, and that particular claims adjuster certainly did, because he didn't have the second step. All he could think about was how he was going to argue with this person. What we'd like to do now is introduce the concept of the empathic connection. It's a very powerful piece. The empathic connection is the difference between what people say and what they mean. Did you hear why he's not getting an estimate? When the customer said, "You guys ran into me, I'm the victim, why should I do your job?" you could have heard two different reasons. You could have heard, "Why should I do your job?" or you could have heard, "I'm the victim here, that's why I'm not doing it." What we want you to do is pay attention to emotional words. The empathic connection is the difference between what someone says and what they mean. Here is an example. Carl actually heard an adjuster one time talking to a customer and the customer said, "Oh man, my brand-new Porsche is creamed." And the adjuster said, "Don't worry, we'll compensate you for the repairs." That sounds kind of normal doesn't it? There's nothing wrong with that. But you know what, that adjuster didn't make the empathic connection and we'll show you what we mean here.

Let us look at another quick example before we do that. Let's say a husband is talking to his wife and the wife says, "Boy, Ivy sure is lucky. Her husband brings her flowers" and the husband says, "She sure is." Obviously, he didn't make the empathic connection. What did she actually mean when she said Ivy sure is lucky? What did she mean? She meant, "*I* would like flowers please," right? But notice that's not what she said. What she said was Ivy is lucky and he says yep, Ivy is lucky. "What's for dinner hun?" He didn't make the empathic connection between what she said and what she meant. Neither did that adjuster who was talking to the customer with the Porsche. Do you think when this customer said, "Oh man, my brand-new Porsche is creamed" that what he was trying to say was, "By the way, will I be compensated for the damages to my automobile?" Probably not. But notice what the adjuster said in response: Don't worry; we'll fix your car. You will be compensated for the repairs. That's not what the customer was really trying to say. That's what he said, but what he meant was, "My life is upside down right now." I mean, he mentions it's a Porsche and he mentions it's brand-new for a reason. What this customer was trying to say was, "My world is out of control right now; I am so upset, I'm beside myself." And had the adjuster heard what the customer meant, instead of just the words, the adjuster could have said something like, "You know what sir, if your brand-new Porsche was creamed, I can understand this is a very difficult situation for you. I am sorry this even happened to you. I can't take the accident back and I am sorry this even happened. What I can do is make sure you get everything you are entitled to and I'll work hard to do that. But I am sorry that this happened." The adjuster could have said that, but he didn't. Do you know why? Because what he heard was, "My car is damaged." Let's go back to our original scenario.

In this case when a customer says, "I'm the victim here; why should I do your job?" you can completely ignore the part where he says, "Why should I do your job?" Pay attention when this person says, "I'm the victim here." See, you need to make the empathic connection between what this person said and what he meant. What this person meant with, "I'm the victim here" is, "I'm the one feeling bad. I'm the one who has been harmed. I need some special help." When people use emotional words like *creamed*, when someone says, "My car got creamed," who knows what happened. Probably the bumper got scratched. But *creamed* is a very emotional word. The word *victim* is also a very emotional word. Think about the word *victim*. What do we normally associate the word *victim* with? We associate it with the victim of a crime. And you know what, he's not too far off. He wasn't doing anything wrong. He was sitting there in his car, we slammed into him, and now he's got to miss a day's work running around getting estimates. For him to feel like a victim is reasonable. What you don't want to do is argue with him. What did we say great negotiators never do? They never argue with reasons. They argue the facts. So, what we might want to do in this case is identify the fact that he's feeling like a victim and get back to the facts at hand.

This is where we would like you to take your shot at this now. We're going to give you a scenario and we want you to take a moment and write down how you would respond. Somebody says to you, "I'm not going to go get that estimate. You guys ran into me. I'm the victim. Why should I do your job?" You know you don't want to argue with the person, and you want to make the empathic connection. What's important right now is this person's feeling like a victim. What would you say to acknowledge his point of view and get back to the facts? Take some time here and give it a try.

We're sure that you came up with a very good response. What we'd like to do now is just add one little extra element, just this little extra bonus item. When you are acknowledging people's point of view, there's one thing you should be aware of. In this case, he's not cooperating because he's feeling like a victim. He's got emotional issues tied up. Here's the thing: If you are trying to change the way people feel, the last thing that will work is arguing with them. You can't talk people out of the way they feel. But you can change the way people feel by acknowledging they are perfectly reasonable for feeling that way. And that's our acknowledgement piece. But there's one extra piece we want to throw in. The more closely you tie in this person changing the way they feel to what you want them to do, the more likely they will do it. We are going to say this again because it's important: The more closely you can tie in this person changing the way they feel to what you want them to do, the more likely they will do it. For this next piece, Doug Baker will again give us a hand. Carl gets to be the adjuster; Doug will be the customer. So as the adjuster, what Carl is going to try to do is tie in changing the way Doug feels to what Carl wants him to do. Carl is going to make that empathic connection but also tie it into the acknowledgement piece.

Customer (Doug Baker): "Hello?"

Adjuster (Carl Van): "Hello, Mr. Baker?"

Customer: "Yes."

Adjuster: "Hi, this is Carl Van with ABC Insurance. How are you?"

AWESOME CLAIMS CUSTOMER SERVICE

Customer: "Fine."

Adjuster: "I'm calling to find out if you can go get an estimate on your car so I can settle your claim."

Customer: "No way!"

Adjuster: "You don't want to do that?"

Customer: "Absolutely not."

Adjuster: "OK, can you tell me why?"

Customer: "I'm the victim here. I'm not doing your job."

Adjuster: "Mr. Baker, if you don't want to go get an estimate because you're feeling like a victim, I can certainly appreciate that. I know you weren't doing anything wrong and our insured ran into you and I am sorry that even happened to you. So, I know this is frustrating for you. I'll tell you what, if you can go get an estimate, a couple of good things will happen to you. First, you'll get to pick the shop, so you can pick the shop you trust. Second, you'll be there when they write the estimate to make sure they don't miss anything. And finally, if you can go get this estimate and get them to send it to me, I can get a check out to you right away. And you know what, maybe when your car is fixed and you're back on the road, maybe you don't have to feel like a victim anymore. That's a lousy way to feel and I would really like to help. Would you go get an estimate so I could help you?"

Customer: "Yeah, I guess so. Can you walk me through it?"

So, is he going to get that estimate? You know, maybe he will and maybe he won't. Our guess is though, that he is much more likely to if we take the time to acknowledge his point of view, especially his feelings, and get back to talking about the facts. And what are those facts? How we can help him. Notice we use the word *help*. Put that in your vocabulary. The best customer service people we have ever seen, especially in claims, use the word *help* often. The best claims people we've ever known say things like, "I'm going to be helping you with your claim," not, "I've been assigned to handle your claim." They don't say, "We have to take depreciation." They say, "Let me help explain why we take depreciation." They use the word *help* a lot. It's a powerful tool.

Remember the three steps to gaining cooperation:

1. When you ask someone to do something and they won't, your first step is to ask why. "Why don't you want to do this? Why are you asking that question?"

Because most of the time, people's reasons for not cooperating have nothing to do with the facts at hand—nothing at all.

2. Acknowledge their point of view. Not that you agree with them. Not that they're right. Just that you understand their point of view. Show them that you think they are a reasonable person.

3. Get back to talking about the facts. Not only the facts of what you want them to do, but the fact you're trying to help them.

These three steps are very powerful. You'll see how to tie them into our next section, which is about getting customers to listen.

CHAPTER 7

Nail Down Questions

This next section has to do with getting customers to listen, and maybe remember. Didn't we say before, our jobs would be so much easier if customers would listen? Well, you know, we're going to get into that. As a matter of fact, we even talked about how nice it would be if customers didn't call us so much. We mentioned before there are certain things we do that make people call us back, even 15 minutes after we talked to them. So, before we get into this, we want to lay the groundwork.

When Carl teaches the Time Management for Claims Adjusters class, he always gets this question: "Carl, how can I possibly return 50 phone calls in a day? How is that possible?"

"You can't possibly return 50 phone calls in a day. You're trying to solve an impossible problem. Meanwhile, you asked the wrong question. Guess what the question should have been? Why am I getting fifty phone calls and what can I do to stop it? That's a much more important question, and I'd rather solve that problem."

One of the reasons we get 50 phone calls is because people aren't listening to us when we are talking. So, wouldn't it be nice if we could get people to listen to us? Also, right now, the way we give information to customers, we almost guarantee that at some point they are not listening, and they can't remember what they're not listening to. So we want to teach you a skill, a very simple concept, that will increase what people will remember we have said from 20 percent to maybe 60 or 70 percent, and make sure they are listening while you are talking.

Although it can happen any time during a claim, most of the time, it happens at the beginning. You're giving someone a lot of information. We're going to do this, you're going to do that, we're going to do this, and you're giving all this information. As soon as you finish this nice big long presentation, what does the customer usually do? Ask questions about what you just said. Then what do you do? Well, you answer those questions. Then what do they do? They ask more questions. What do you do?

You answer those questions. Guess what? You're playing ping-pong back and forth. Right now, that's happening because people aren't really listening, and they certainly don't remember what we're saying. We have to figure out why that's happening and see if we can solve it. You know what? There's hope. We promise. It's coming up right now. We are going to teach you how to increase retention from 20 to maybe 60 or 70 percent on the customer's part, and make sure he or she is listening while you are talking.

Teresa Headrick, one of our trainers, will be our adjuster in our next scenario. In this situation, Carl is going to be the customer and Teresa is going to explain to Carl, as we all do, what is going to happen in the claims process. Now, just to be brief, we are going to skip the part of the whole conversation where she's asking Carl all the questions about the loss and we're going to get to the part of the claim where we tend to give customers a lot of information because, believe it or not, that's when they stop listening.

Adjuster (Teresa Headrick): "Well Carl, now that I've gotten all the information that I need from you, what I'm going to do is tell you what's going to happen next."

Customer (Carl Van): "OK."

Adjuster: "I am going to send an appraiser out and they are going to be writing an estimate on the damages to your home. They will look at the damages in your kitchen and also in your bathroom. They will prepare that estimate and leave you a copy of it. Also, they will send a copy to me for my review for payment. Once you get the payment from me, you can contact any contractor you'd like of your choice, give them that estimate, if they have any questions on it, first they'll call the appraiser and then the appraiser will call me to go over what additional damages the contractor etc. etc. etc."

Teresa did a great job there. Probably sounded familiar didn't it? We tend to give people a lot of information. Did you notice how many items of information Teresa was providing? If you count up the number of facts Teresa provided, it comes up to something like 15 or 16: send someone out; write an estimate; etc. She's not done yet. She's still got a long way to go to give Carl all the information he needs. So, we're at 15 on our way to 50, no problem.

Most psychologists say if you give information this way— fact, fact, fact, fact—by the time you're done, the person you are talking to is going to remember about 20 percent of what you said. What's the proof of that? What happens as soon as you give people a lot of information? What do they turn around and do? Ask you questions. Usually, about what? About what you just said. So right now, the way we tend to give information in claims—a lot of facts—the customer is remembering about 20 percent of what we tell them. What if there was a way we could push that up to 60 or 70 percent? Would that make your job easier? You bet it would.

Before we teach you that, we've got another question for you. Let's say that Teresa is giving Carl information and she's going to send someone out to his house and let's say for some reason, Carl doesn't want anybody coming to his house. Who knows? Maybe he got robbed three years ago. What happens in Carl's mind when Teresa says, "OK, we're going to assign this to an appraiser who's going to come out to your house, write an estimate on your house, and give you a copy..." What happened in Carl's mind as soon as she said, "We're coming out to your house?" That's right - he stopped listening. He's not listening to anything she's saying. You know what he's doing while she's talking? He is formulating his reply. However, Teresa doesn't know that so she's still talking. She'll find out because when she says, "Do you have any questions?" Carl will bring her right back to the point where he stopped listening.

Wouldn't it be nice if we knew when people stopped listening? Well, you know what, you should have this skill. As a claims adjuster (or any another professional) your job is to give information to customers. Your job is to make sure they understand you. Shouldn't you have a tool that allows you to know when someone stops listening? What if we could teach you a way that would automatically tell you when someone stops listening? Would that tool be valuable? Well, we're going to do that too. Getting people to remember more of what you said and knowing when they stop listening are both tied up in a concept, we call *nail down questions*.

As far as listening goes, one thing we need to appreciate in claims is basically there are two times when customers stop listening. The first time is when you are giving people information and you say something they object to such as sending someone out to their house. The second time people stop listening is if you use a word they don't understand or some concept or term of insurance they can't comprehend.

Here is a question for you: What are the odds that Teresa can give Carl 50 facts in a row, in a process he doesn't understand and he's nervous and scared about, and not use a single word he doesn't understand and not say a single thing he objects to? What are the odds of this, do you think? Probably pretty low, right? So, the way we give information right now to customers, we're almost guaranteeing at some point, they're not listening. We're going to be able to solve that with the nail down questions.

As we get into nail down questions, one very important item we have to understand is this: When we give people a lot of information in a row, many memory and psychology experts tell us people can only hold two, maybe three, facts in their conscious mind at any given time. It's not how many things can you remember, but how many things can you think of at the same time. For most of us, it's two, maybe three. When Teresa was talking to Carl, how many did he get in a row? He got 15. Many psychologists will tell us that if you do this, what people can remember works like first-in first-out inventory. The first fact comes in, no problem. The second fact comes in, no problem. The third fact comes in, what happens to the first one? Gone. Number four comes in, what happens to number two? Gone. Number five comes in, what happens to number three? Gone. And you're just shifting information—unless you can force the person to make a judgment on the information as you go. If you can force someone to think about and respond to information as you go, they're much more likely to remember it because you have engaged them. This is a very important concept for us.

A nail down question is any question to which the answer is *yes*. Just a simple question. You with me? Make sense? Sound OK? Any question you can get the person to say *yes* to is a nail down question. We're going to insert that question every two, three, or four facts when we're talking to customers, just to involve them. Notice what that does. That forces them to make a judgment on the information as we go. And if we do that, instead of twenty percent, they are going to remember sixty or seventy percent of what we say because we've involved them. We've forced them to make a judgment on the information as we go. And there's an added bonus. We're also going to find out when they stop listening, which we're going to show you. This time, Teresa is going to be the customer and Carl gets to be the adjuster, and he's going to show you how nail down questions do a great job in the claims environment of getting a customer to listen to us and remember what we say. We will make the scenario an auto claim. Carl is going to explain the process near the end of the conversation and see if he can't throw in a nail down question every two, three, or four, facts.

Adjuster (Carl Van): "OK Teresa, well now that I've gotten all the information from you that I need, let me go ahead and explain how the process is going to work. Is that alright?"

Customer (Teresa Headrick): "Sure."

Adjuster: "The very first thing we are going to do is, we are going to send someone out to write an estimate on your car, give you a copy of that estimate and you can take that estimate to any body shop you'd like. Make sense?"

Customer: "Yes it does."

Adjuster: "OK, good, once you go ahead and give the estimate to the body shop, have them check it, if there's any questions, have them call me or the person who wrote the estimate. Sound good?"

Customer: "Yeah."

Adjuster: "OK, good. Once they go ahead and are getting your car fixed, if you need a rental car, now you said you didn't need one, but if you do, call me and I can set up a direct bill, that way you don't have to lay out any cash. Does that sound good?"

Customer: "Yeah it does."

Adjuster: "Alright, good. Now as far as your medical information goes…"

Did you see what happened as Carl was talking? He's just throwing in a nail down question for every two or three facts. Just little things like, "Does that sound good? Is that ok with you? Is that alright?" Just little things to get her to respond. Notice what's happening? Every time she says yes, his information goes down to long-term memory, it clears up his conscious mind for the next few facts and now Carl can move on. Is Teresa ever going

AWESOME CLAIMS CUSTOMER SERVICE

to remember 100 percent of what Carl tells her? Is that possible? No. But we have to tell you, 60 or 70 percent is a whole world better than 20 percent because 20 percent is what the customer is remembering right now.

So, Teresa made that pretty easy on Carl, didn't she? She just kept saying yes, as he was talking, but customers don't always say yes. Sometimes they say no. Is a reply of "No" a bad thing? No, because we said something either the customer objected to or didn't understand, and we might as well find out now rather than waiting. So, the nice thing about nail down questions is it lets you check in with the customer. If Carl were to say to Teresa, "Does that sound good? Does that make sense?" and Teresa says, "No," what question do we want to ask? "What doesn't sound good? What doesn't make sense?" We might as well solve the problem now because we know one thing: Teresa's not going to listen anymore.

A nice side benefit of using the nail down questions is that it lets you know when someone's not listening. For example, let's say you're talking and you're giving information and you say, "Does that sound good?" Don't be surprised when a customer says, "Does what sound good?" Keep in mind, they may not be listening, and now, when you're asking them, "Does that sound good?" you're forcing them into the conversation. So, don't be surprised if this actually happens. As a matter of fact, you might even expect it. Don't be insulted. Just repeat yourself and pretty soon, after you ask that question a couple of times, "Does that sound good? Does that make sense?" they will get used to the fact that you are asking these questions and guess what — they will pay attention to you. It's a great customer service focused, very polite way to let a customer know what you're telling them is important, and they will listen.

So, let's give this a try. In this case, Teresa will again be the customer and Carl is going to be the claims adjuster. We'll make it an injury claim or something like that. And Carl is going to do his best to use nail down questions. At some point, she is going to say no, and Carl has to do his best to respond to it.

Adjuster (Carl Van): "Alright, well Teresa, now that I've got this information, let me explain how the process is going to work. The very first thing we are going to do is we are going to send out a medical authorization form, I need you to sign that form and send it back into me. Sound alright?"

Customer (Teresa Headrick): "That's fine."

Adjuster: "OK, once I get that form, I'll send it to your doctors, get a full medical history, along with the bills and I will review them. Sound good?"

AWESOME CLAIMS CUSTOMER SERVICE

Customer: "No."

Adjuster: "No, it doesn't sound good? Well, what doesn't sound good to you?"

Customer: "A full medical history, you are going to get everything I've ever done in my entire life with a doctor?"

Adjuster: "I'm sorry. What I meant was a medical history for this particular accident, along with the bills that are related to this accident. Does that sound good?"

Customer: "Yeah, that's OK."

Adjuster: "OK, good. Once I get all of that, I review them, of course, and then I submit them for payment and I will contact you to let you know which ones and how much we are going to be paying. Does that sound good?"

Customer: "Yeah, it sure does."

Adjuster: "OK, good."

Notice what happened here. Teresa did throw in a no. Carl said something she objected to and what happened? Carl had to find out what it was, solve the problem, and keep talking. What would have happened had Carl not asked that question? He would have been talking, and she wouldn't have been listening. And there's no value in that.

Carl was teaching a customer service class once and the class all went out to lunch and the waiter came up to the group and said, "You guys want to hear about the special?" "Yeah, yeah," they replied, "tell us about the special." So he went through the process, "Well it's this pasta and it's got this sauce, it's got this and it's got this and it's got this and it's got this and it's got this and it's got leeks and it's got hazelnuts and it's got cheese." And they all said, "Oh wow, that sounds really good. You know, maybe I'll have that." So, Carl turned to the person next to him and said, "So, what does that have on it again?" And he said, "Leeks and cheese, I think." The only thing he could remember were the last couple of things this guy said. Why? Because the facts are just coming along, going in, going out, and basically, he could remember about twenty percent of what that waiter said. Carl asked the whole table what the pasta was, and nobody could even remember what kind of pasta it was and that was the whole dish. Nail down questions do a great job of getting customers to listen and remember what we say. But there is something else about nail down questions we want to talk about.

Nail down questions, like we mentioned, are for when you are the one doing all the talking. So, if you are just asking questions and they are answering them, you really don't need them. But you also have to understand something. This is only to get people to remember what you said and listen to you. Don't try to use nail down questions to convince people you are right. It doesn't work. We'll give you a real-life example. Carl had a student call him one time after a training class. He said, "Carl, I love the nail down questions. They really work. I get a lot less questions. I get a lot of fewer phone calls. But they don't always work." Carl said, "Well, what do you mean they don't always work?" And he said, "I was talking to my wife." And Carl said, "Uh oh, what happened?" He said, "Every Friday we go out to dinner then afterward we do something; either we go bowling or we go to the movies. I like to go bowling. She likes to go to the movies. So, I figured I'd use the nail down questions." Carl could see it coming but kept listening. "OK," Carl said, "what happened?" He said, "I called her up at work and I said 'Honey, we're going to go to dinner this Friday night. We are going to go to the restaurant you picked out, but afterward, we're going to go bowling. Are you with me so far?'" Needless to say, it didn't go too well. So, remember, nail down question aren't for convincing someone you're right; they for getting someone to remember what you said.

What you don't want to do is continually repeat yourself if they don't understand or agree with something you said. So, if you were to say something like, "We're going to send you a medical form. I'd like you to sign it and send it back. Does that sound good?" "No." "OK, see, there's this medical form and you have to sign it and send it back in. Does that make sense?" "No." "OK, see we have this form, and it's called a medical authorization." Rather than repeating yourself over and over again, find out what they don't understand. So, if the response to a nail down question is "no," what you want to say is, "Well, what doesn't sound good? What doesn't make sense? What is it you're not with me about?" Use the exact same words you used to ask the question. What you don't want to do is imply they don't understand. If you say, "Well, what don't you understand?" you could insult some people because now you're calling them stupid. So, use the exact same words you used to ask the initial question. Alright, what we want to do now is set up an exercise for you.

So now it's time to practice. We do understand without a partner, it might not be easy but it's not impossible. You can go ahead and do it. Think of a situation where you give a lot of information to customers. Remember, we don't need nail down questions if you're asking questions and they are answering them. That's not necessary. This is for when you're doing a lot of talking. You could be a total loss adjuster explaining how the total loss process works. You could be a slip and fall adjuster talking to

AWESOME CLAIMS CUSTOMER SERVICE

someone about how you are going to analyze injuries. You could be a construction defect adjuster talking about how you're going to analyze coverage. It doesn't matter. We want you to think of a scenario where you do a lot of explaining and give a lot of information and what we want you to do is practice using nail down questions. Go ahead and say it out loud and practice giving information, every two or three facts, throwing in a nail down question, and seeing if you can get all the way through. While you're doing this, you might experience one difficulty with nail down questions. You see, we tend to memorize things in order. And now we are inserting something that's not in that order. And you know what might happen? You might forget where you were. Just as you're talking and you ask your pretend partner, "Does that make sense?" and they say, "Yes," you might forget where you were. You can overcome this problem very easily with a little bit of practice, which is what we're going to do now. But don't be surprised if you forget where you were; it does happen. So, take some time and think of a scenario. Plan what you are going to say then go ahead and use some nail down questions and practice giving this a try.

How did you do? Maybe it went well. Maybe it didn't go so well. That's OK. It all gets better with practice. We promise. If you have somebody that you can grab and say, "Hey, let me try this on you," by all means go ahead and do it. Maybe show them how to do it and you can help somebody else while you're at it. Practice is the name of the game. Remember, *as you practice, so shall you do.* Don't get discouraged if it doesn't work the first time.

Before we move on to another topic, we need to discuss why we solicit the answer *yes*. We get this question quite a bit. One important reason we ask yes questions (rather than no questions) is because human beings remember better when they agree rather than disagree. A positive yes question increases the likelihood of retention. In addition, yes questions put people in the mood of agreement. If you were to say, "Do you have a problem with that?" and they say, "No," you're still getting the benefit of a nail down question because you're involving the customer. Nevertheless, try to stick with positive questions like "Make sense?" or "Sound good?"

Listed below are five benefits of using nail down questions.

1. A nail down question allows you to check in with a customer after only a few pieces of information to make sure they understand.

2. Since the answer to these questions should be yes, it will help a customer associate positively with

your explanation and hopefully they will remember more facts, or at least your explanation.

3. If customers remember more of what you're willing to tell them about the claims process, chances are they will feel better about it and ask fewer questions.

4. If a customer is not prepared to answer yes, at least you'll find out early in the conversation and resolve issues right away.

5. Explaining and nailing down a smaller bit of information is more efficient and effective customer service. You won't waste time telling customers things after they've tuned out because they're still focused on something you said earlier they didn't agree with.

CHAPTER 8

The Voice Mail Multiplier

Well, so far in this book, we've talked about a lot of things that should make our jobs easier and improve customer service. Let's go back, just for a second, for a quick review.

Nail down questions should make our job easier, but do they improve customer service? Well, think about it. If customers are listening while we are talking, and they remember more of what we say, there's a good chance they're not going to have to call us back, which is a burden on them. They will also feel better informed.

How about the three steps for negotiating for cooperation? If we do a good job of identifying a customer's issues and acknowledging their point of view, they will feel better understood and again, customer service goes up. In addition, our job becomes easier.

Well, we said before it would make our job easier if people didn't call us so much. Remember that? Well now we are going to learn a customer service skill, one or two, that should improve customer service but also make our job easier by getting customers to not call so much.

We mentioned before that in our time management classes, we get the question, "How could I return fifty phone calls?" and what did we say the response was? What are we doing to get fifty phone calls? That's what we need to focus on and that's something we'd like to address right now. In that time management class, it takes a full day, but we shift people's focus from what they think is important to what's a priority. For us in claims we must focus on priorities, because we work in an environment where we can't get all of the work done. Many times, identifying what is a priority and what isn't can be a difficult task. But, if you identify them properly, you definitely can save yourself some time.

Let us give you a hint. One of the things we teach in our time management class is anything that will take longer to do later than now is a priority. We know that's a difficult shift, so we want to give it to you again. *Anything that will take longer to do later than now is a priority.* This maxim is true in claims because we can't get all of our work done. If everything we did now took less time than if we did it later, what would we have more of later? Time. And this is a perfect example of what we're going to teach you. It's called the *voice mail multiplier.* Let's say you're sitting at your desk. You're working on something. It's very complicated. You're focused, and you don't want to be disturbed. The phone rings, and guess what you do. You let the call roll into voice mail. Why? Because you want to be efficient; you don't want to lose your focus. We often make this choice. However, let's take a look at the impact of this decision.

The standard number of calls handled by a claims professional in a week is about 200. If you're a call center person, you're going to handle a lot more. If you're a field representative, you're going to handle a lot less. Nevertheless, we're going use the figure of 200 for this example. Let's say you were at your desk and you have 200 phone calls and you answer every single one of them. Of course, you can't do that because you're on the phone sometimes and sometimes you're not even there. But let's say you could. If you answered every single phone call that comes in, how many phone calls would you have? You'd have 200, right? But let's say you made a different decision. Let's say you decided you're not going to answer any phone calls. They all go to voice mail. Let's look at that.

AWESOME CLAIMS CUSTOMER SERVICE

So now you have 200 phone calls that roll into voice mail. What do you have to do with those 200 phone calls? You've got to return them. Not 100 percent. Most time management experts will tell you that only about 90 percent you actually have to return. The other 10 percent were calls just providing some information you needed. So now you've got to make 180 outgoing phone calls. Do you get all 180 of these people? No. You get about half. So, you will talk to 90, and you will leave a message for the other 90. What do these 90 people do when they get your message? Well, 90 percent will call you back. So now you have 81 phone calls coming in. Of course, what happens? They roll into voice mail. What do you have to do with these 81 phone calls? You've got to return them—not 100 percent but 90 percent. So now you've got to make 72 outgoing phone calls. Do you get all 72 of these people? No, you get about half, so you talk to 36 and you leave a message for 36. What do these 36 people do when they get your message? Well, 90 percent of them will call you back. So now you get 33 phone calls. And, of course, what happens? They roll into voice mail. What do you have to do with these 33 phone calls? You've got to return them—not 100 percent but 90 percent. So now you have to make 30 outgoing phone calls. Do you get all 30 of these people? No, you get about half. So, you talk to 15 and... We think you know where we're going.

So, guess what? By the time this is all done (and by the way, this is called the voice mail multiplier) you have somewhere between 600 and 800 total phone calls. Now we have had people say, "Well, I don't get 600 phone calls." No, because you answer your phone, thank goodness. But the average is three to four additional phone calls for every call that you could have answered but didn't. Think about this: For every call that you could have answered but for whatever reason, decided not to, you've actually generated three to four additional phone calls. You've created work that didn't even exist but for the fact you choose not to answer your phone. Why did you choose not to answer your phone? To be more efficient? To maintain your focus? That's all fine and good. But you have to understand the impact of your decision. What's a priority? Anything that will take more time to do later than now is a priority. Well, how do you make that decision? You don't even know what the call coming in is about. Well, that's the old standard of trying to figure out which is more important. You don't know what's more important, the phone call or what you are working on. But you do know one thing about the phone call. If you don't answer it, you will generate three to four additional phone calls later. You are generating work that didn't even exist until you made that decision.

Now, you know there are some people you are going to get right away when you call them back. Some people, you are going to play telephone tag with 12 times, you know this. But the average is still three to four phone calls being generated every time you didn't answer a call when you could have. Now if you can't answer a call because you're not there or you can't answer a call because you're on the phone, don't feel bad about that. There's nothing you could have done. But you know what, if you don't answer a phone call when you could have, you must understand the impact of that decision. Now, if you're working on something, that's admirable. But let's say you've got a co-worker walking up and saying, "Hey, did you see that football game last night? Did you see what happened?" And you say, "No, what happened?" Then the phone rings, and you have a decision to make: Do I stand here and listen to this person or do I answer this call? One of these two choices is going to generate work for you. And one of them is going to reduce the amount of work you have. Which choice are you going to make? So, you make that choice. We don't want to tell you what to do. But we do want to add one more thing about the voice mail multiplier you should understand.

Sometimes we use voice mail as a crutch. We don't want to answer the phone. We're stressed out. We don't want to talk to whoever is calling in. So, we use it as a crutch to deal with stress. We want to address that issue, just for a second. We'll give you some examples. You might be at your desk and a co-worker walks up to you and says, "Oh, you wouldn't believe this jerk that just talked to me. Oh, I can't believe what this guy just said!" You stop what you are doing so you can listen. Why do we dump our problems on each other? Well, many people say it relieves stress. It gets it off our chest. Well, this is where the stress management experts step in and say, "no it doesn't." You are just trading it for the stress you are going to feel at the end of the day when you don't have your work done. You're not relieving anything. You're just moving it back and it's going to be in a different form because now you've got more work to do. Meanwhile, guess what? Your phone is ringing. In order to be polite, you don't answer it. Now, your co-worker is generating more work for those around him or her.

The voice mail multiplier is a very powerful thing. When the phone rings, do what you can to answer it. Because right now, we are generating work in order to save ourselves work and that doesn't make a lot of sense. That's just one example of the things we can do to get customers to not call us so much.

So why do we get 50 phone calls? Well one reason is because we don't use nail down questions. And customers are calling us back just a few minutes after we talk to them. Another reason is because we don't answer the phone when we have the chance and the voice mail multiplier kicks in and starts generating work. There's a third reason we get a lot of phone calls and that has to do with just the way we talk to customers. As a matter of fact, even the way we end a conversation. If you knew that by ending a conversation a certain way, you were encouraging people to call you back a few minutes later, would you do it? Most people wouldn't. But you're going to find out that it's a very common thing we do in claims. Let's say you're at the end of a phone call. You've talked to somebody, let's say you've even used nail down questions and got all of the information out. At the end of the call, before you hang up, we always say, "Did you have any more questions?" And if the person says, "Yes, I have more questions," you have to answer them. And if the person says no, well, guess what, you get to hang up. But guess what a lot of us do: We end the conversation with, "Do you have any more questions?" "No." "OK, well if you get any more questions, ..." What? "Call me." Well, that's just customer service. We are just trying to be polite. And that's true, it is being polite. But from a customer service standpoint, think about this: Anything that you do that makes the customer have to call you back when they didn't have to, well, guess what, that's not great customer service. Does that statement really have such a big impact? Well, think about it. The person is on the other end of the phone. You've just said, "Do you have any more questions?" and they said no. You say, "Well, if you get any more questions..." What are you focusing this person on? Questions. And when you say, "Well, call me if you have any more questions," they're hanging up the phone going, click, "Do I have any more questions?" And since you just focused their attention on it, guess what they are going to see? They are going to see questions. Does it really have this impact? We'll show you how it has this impact.

Here's what we want you to do. We know it's going to seem strange but just humor us. We want you to look around the room wherever you might happen to be sitting. Just look around the room. And look for anything that might be blue. Anything at all. Any shade of blue. Take a good look around. We're going to test your observation skills. Go ahead and take a look around. Now what we want you to do is to close your eyes. Go ahead, close them. Now while your eyes are closed, we want you to think of anything you just saw that was red. Go ahead and open your eyes. Did you find that difficult? Were you able to do it easily or was it tough? Well a lot of people would say it was difficult. Well, why? There's red probably all around you. "Well, because I was focused on blue." Ahh.... Exactly.

You were focused on blue because we focused you on blue. People see what they are looking for. Human beings are pretty simple creatures. We see what we're looking for. Sometimes, we'll miss everything else around us because we are looking for something intently enough. And we focused you on blue. We could get you to see anything we want, red, green, blue, triangles, circles, squares, it doesn't matter. Whatever we tell you to look for, you are going to see. And you are going to miss most other things. When you're on the phone with someone, and you say, "Do you have any more questions?" and they say no, and you say, "Well, if you get any more questions..." what are you focusing them on? Questions. And when you say, "If you get any more questions give me a call," what are you focusing them on? Questions. And you are, quite literally, leaving the conversation with their total focus on questions. And believe us, they are on the other end of the phone going, "Do I have any more questions?" And since you just focused them on that, guess what they see? They see questions. And by the way, what did you tell them to do when they found questions? Call you.

Does it really have this impact? Well, have you ever known anybody with a really bad attitude? It doesn't matter what you say. "Hey, it's sunny outside." "I'll get sunburned." "Well, maybe it will rain then." "I just washed my car." "Hey, we are going to give you a big fat raise." "No, more taxes, I don't want it." You know there are some people, no matter what you say, they will see the bad in it. These aren't bad people; they're just seeing what they are looking for. What you have is the opportunity to focus people on what you want them to see. What you don't want them to see is more questions. So, right now, the way we end a conversation, we're quite literally encouraging them to look for questions. Our suggestion is to simply not end the conversation with this sentence. You can say it. Just don't make it the last thing you say. So, you are on the phone with somebody and you say, "Do you have any more questions?" They say, "No, I don't have any more questions." It's perfectly OK for you to say, "Well, you know what, if you have any more questions, I want you to feel free to call me at any time. Does that sound good?" "Yeah, OK good." "Before I let you go, let me just remind you that I will be calling you on Friday when I get that estimate." "OK, alright, goodbye." Guess what you've just focused them on: that you're going to be calling them on Friday. Guess what you haven't focused them on: questions.

We don't want to change company policy for you. If somebody tells you, "From now on, you're required to always end the conversation with _____" by all means, do it. But if there's a way that you could change the way you do things just a little bit so you can still make the statement but just don't make it the last thing you say, you'll be much better off. And by the way, this is a one hundred percent spoken cue. If at the bottom of your letters, it says, "Please call us if you have any questions," it doesn't mean a thing. It has no impact. This is a one hundred percent spoken cue. So, here's what we'd like you to try. We know it's going to seem odd, but we want you to practice this. What we want you to do right now is see if you could practice ending the conversation

AWESOME CLAIMS CUSTOMER SERVICE

without making, "Call me if you have any questions" the last thing you say. You can say it, just don't make it the last thing you say. Are you ready to try it? Go ahead.

CHAPTER 9

Overcoming the Question after Question Cycle

We said before it would make our job easier if people would just trust us. Well, why is it our customers sometimes don't trust us? Sometimes we use the wrong words, which we are going to talk about. Sometimes it's just the way we give information. But we do have to listen *better*. We mentioned before, the empathic connection: the difference between what someone's saying and what they mean. This next exercise is going to tie all of these in together because if we could pay attention to when customers are being nervous and anxious and want some reassurance, instead of just giving them words back, we might be able to give them back what they really need, which is some reassurance that someone's watching out for them.

This chapter also involves a little bit of role play, some exercise on your part, and what we want to do is see if we can build trust in a relationship between us and our customer and make our job a little bit easier. This role play involves a customer who tends to ask a lot of questions. Have you ever had a customer like that—someone who asks question after question after question? We call it the *question after question cycle.* And right now, the only thing we know to do is just to answer every single question the person has, which is nice, it's kind of good customer service, but it doesn't really get to the issue at hand. What we want to do is see if we can reduce the amount of time we have to use in order to deal with that situation and improve customer service.

For this next role play, Teresa is going to play the claims professional. Jon is going to play the customer. We want you to see if you can tell what is it that Jon is doing that should be a good indicator to Teresa that Jon is nervous and anxious. See if you can spot it. Now, what she's going to do is she's going to start off the conversation as if he is trying to end it and say something along the lines of, "Mr. Coscia, do you have any more questions?" And we know that if we ask that question, "Do you have any more questions?" and the person says no, we get to hang up. But if the person says yes, guess what we have to do? We have to work to answer the questions. Let's see how this goes. In this case, we're basically ending the conversation; all you have to do is ask the golden question: "Mr. Coscia, do you have any more questions?" and we will go from there.

Claims professional (Teresa Headrick): "Mr. Coscia, do you have any more questions?"

Customer (Jon Coscia): "Yeah, I have a question. What if the body shop runs out of parts when they are fixing my car? What happens then?"

Claims professional: "Well, that probably won't happen, but if it does, I will call them, and we will go over our process for dealing with body shops and running out of parts."

Customer: "OK, well you said I had to give a statement, but you said you had to record it. I mean, why do you guys have to record these things? Why can't you just write them out?"

Claim professional: "Mr. Coscia, that's so we can preserve your statement so that in case the story changes from one party to the other, we'll have that information preserved."

AWESOME CLAIMS CUSTOMER SERVICE

Customer: "Does that happen a lot, people change their stories?"

Claims professional: "Well, no, not frequently, but in case it does, we'll have your statement preserved on the recording."

Customer: "Well, I would think a written statement would be more a preservation of evidence than recorded."

Claims professional: "Well, it's true, Mr. Coscia, the written would also preserve the evidence, but we like to use the recordings because we can actually hear what the person is saying."

Customer: "Well, ahh, let's see, how about that medical form. You said I had to sign a medical form in order to get the bills. Why can't you just write to my doctor and get the bills? How come I have to sign some dumb form?"

Claims professional: "Oh, Mr. Coscia, please understand there are federal laws which require that we protect your privacy and that's why we have to have that."

Customer: "Well, why don't the insurance companies get together and have a bill passed where you don't have to do that kind of stuff?"

Claims professional: "Mr. Coscia, I don't know why."

Teresa did a great job there, didn't she? Didn't that conversation sound familiar with question after question after question after question? This is what we know how to do when people are nervous and anxious. But here's what we didn't notice. Teresa is going to do her best job as a customer service professional to answer every question Jon has. Let's go back to the empathic connection, the difference between what someone says and what they mean. When someone is asking question after question after question, do you think what they really want is to know every single thing about the claims process there is to know? Do you think that's what they want? Probably not. What is it that they want? Well, think about it. When people ask question after question after question, it probably means they are very nervous, and they are anxious. When people are very nervous and anxious, they don't really need to know everything about the claims process. They need something else.

What they probably need is some reassurance, on our part, that we are reasonably intelligent people who know that this is important, and we are going to try to do a good job for them. When people ask question after question after question after question, what you should be hearing is, "I'm very nervous and anxious." Then you don't have to waste time giving them a bunch of

AWESOME CLAIMS CUSTOMER SERVICE

information, which you have already admitted they don't want. In order to do that, we have a five-step process for you. It's pretty simple; we are going to go through all five steps. We are going to learn them as we go through the role plays.

To solve the question after question cycle, we have to have an appreciation for the types of questions people tend to ask when they are nervous and anxious. If somebody asks you, "What's my deductible, where should I get this thing fixed" etc., these aren't nervous and anxious questions. These are questions they need answered. But when people start asking you, "What about this, and, how come that, and, how come insurance companies don't get together and do these things," they're asking questions because they're uncomfortable with the claims process. People ask nervous and anxious questions basically for two reasons. Number one: they're not comfortable with the claims process. So, what do we do? We answer questions. But number two: they're asking question after question after question because they're not comfortable with who? With us. They don't know to ask questions about us. They are trying to get a level of credibility and trust out of us, but they don't know how to do that. So, guess what they keep asking questions about: the claims process. And they keep doing that, we keep answering it and believe it or not, the more we answer it, the more it feeds into the process. What we have to do is understand where our credibility comes from. We think our credibility comes from the fact we know everything. We can quote the policy. We have lots of experience. Most customer service experts will tell you this is not where your credibility comes from. It comes from some place very different.

Your credibility comes from your ability to demonstrate you understand where the other person is coming from. We know this might seem odd. But remember our other maxim: People will consider your point of view to the exact degree you demonstrate you understand theirs. Well, this is very close to that. Your credibility does not come from how brilliant you are or how much you can quote the policy or case law. Believe it or not, when people are nervous and anxious, which many of our customers are, your credibility comes from your ability to demonstrate you understand where the other person is coming from. To illustrate this phenomenon, we are going to take Teresa out of the claims world. Let's say Teresa is sick, or she is going in for an operation. Jon happens to be her surgeon, and he believes people should trust him because he knows a lot. Jon is going to talk to Teresa about the operation. We'll see how he does as far as gaining trust.

Surgeon (Jon Coscia): "Teresa, I'm going to be your surgeon on this operation. I hope it goes well. Here's what we're going to do. We're going to cut you open here, we're going to tie this, we're going to pull this out, we're going to sew you back up, we're going to send you off to the ICU, you're going to have lots of symptoms and if you have any questions, you just ask. So, Teresa, before we do this, you got any questions?"

Patient (Teresa Headrick): "Oh, you bet I do!"

Teresa's going to have some questions, like, "Who's your malpractice carrier?" Or, "Where's the exit?" She's going to have a lot of questions. As a surgeon, Jon tries to rely on the fact that he knows a lot, and he's going to answer every single question Teresa has. At the end, Jon is going to hope for some level of trust and credibility. But let's try this again. Let's say Jon doesn't believe that. Let's say, as a surgeon, he believes that his credibility comes from his ability to demonstrate he understands where Teresa is coming from. Let's just say Jon believes that, and he takes a different approach. Again, Jon is Teresa's surgeon, maybe it's an emergency, who knows?

Surgeon (Jon Coscia): "Alright, Teresa, I'm going to be your surgeon on this operation, and I know you have lots of questions, we'll get to those in a second. Before we get started, I'd like to mention just a couple of things. First, for this operation to go very smoothly, I understand that's important to you. I understand that to start. You may be a little nervous, you may be a little anxious, and you know what, that's perfectly normal. Most people are. Don't even worry about that. I know this is new for you, but I've been doing this operation for many, many years. I have an extremely high success rate, that's why they called me. I can't promise the world or that everything is going to go perfectly. But I can tell you, I'm going to do everything I can to make sure that this operation does go smoothly because I understand how important it is, especially to you. Does that sound alright?"

Patient (Teresa Headrick): "Yeah."

Surgeon: "Ok, good, now let's get to those questions."

So, is Teresa going to be Ms. Sunshine now? Is she going to be running around saying, "Oh boy, am I glad I'm going to have an operation now!" Probably not. And she's going to have some questions, which is good. But we want you to notice something. Is there a chance that Teresa might have a little bit more trust in Jon the second time than the first time? Is there just a chance she has some level of trust in the second scenario she never had in the first scenario? Probably. And we want you to notice something very important: Jon has not said a single word about the operation yet in the second scenario. Not a single word. Jon hasn't even mentioned how it's going to go. Yet, he already has more credibility than the first surgeon will ever get. Why? Because your credibility doesn't come from how much you know. It doesn't come from how smart you are. Your credibility comes from your ability to demonstrate you understand where other people are coming from. This we lose sight of in claims, but it's a powerful tool.

So, remember, the strategy for stopping the question after question cycle (*the customer service strategy*) consists of five steps.

1. Acknowledge. Acknowledge the importance of the process to the customer.

2. Empathy. Empathize with the customer's feelings but don't be too intrusive.

3. Permission. Give the customer permission to worry or feel bad. Let them know their feelings are normal.

4. Experience. Make a modest comment about your experience.

5. Promise. See if you can tie the empathic statement into a promise that you will use your experience to do everything you can to make the process go well.

What we'd like to do is go over the five steps, and we hope you noticed there was a process here of trying to gain credibility by using the idea that our credibility comes from our ability to demonstrate we understand where the other person is coming from. If we do this in claims, it's very powerful. The first step is what we call the acknowledgement step; to acknowledge that you understand this is important to that person. If we were to say to a customer, "We understand this is important to you," what happens to your credibility? Does it go up or does it go down? It goes up. When you say something very true to a customer, your credibility goes up.

Then what was the next thing Jon said? He used a little bit of empathy. That's step number two. "You might be nervous. You might be anxious. A lot of people are." And then step number three, which is permission. "Don't worry about it. Most people are." Combine those two. "You might be nervous and anxious." That's showing a little empathy. "Don't worry about it, most people are." What happens when you tell a customer being nervous and anxious is perfectly normal? What happens to their level of anxiety? It goes down. They're not dancing in the street but they're a little calmer than they were. "You might be nervous and anxious, if you are, don't worry about it. Most people are."

Step number four is experience. Notice what Jon said, "This may be new for you, but I have been doing this operation for a number of years now and I have an extremely high success rate." What you don't want to do is brag. "I've been doing this for twenty-five years and you've got nothing to worry about." Bragging makes you lose credibility, but to make a modest statement about your experience so someone knows you have some experience is helpful. However, you need to tie it into step number five, which is promise.

The promise step is the last and probably the most important step. Can this surgeon promise that everything is going to go perfectly? Is that possible? No, he can't promise that. But what did he promise? He promised that he was going to do everything he could to make sure that it does go well. You know what he just promised to do? He promised to do his job. His job as a surgeon is to do whatever it takes to make sure this operation goes smoothly. It's a very powerful statement to let someone know we're going to do whatever it takes to make something go right. We have that opportunity in claims, and we want to share with you a true story about how this works.

Every once in a while, Carl will get students saying, "Well, Carl, this is all good, but I deal in the real world. I don't have time to spoon feed people." Carl's response is that this *is* the real world; these five steps came from a situation he heard. When Carl was a brand-new claims representative, he was having a tough time. He liked his job, but he was getting into arguments with people. They were calling him back 20 minutes after he talked to them, asking question after question after question. This was going on for a while. Meanwhile, there was another claim representative named Drew. He never got in fights, and customers hardly ever called him. So, Carl decided to sit with Drew and see what he was doing that Carl was not. So, Carl spent an entire day with Drew, listening to what he said to people. The stuff Drew used to say absolutely blew Carl away.

When Drew would get a customer that would ask question after question after question, instead of wearing them out with bunch of answers like Carl would, he would actually say something along the lines of this, "You know what, those are some pretty good questions. Let me interrupt you just for a second and mention something just real briefly. I can see by these questions that for this claim to go smoothly is very important to you. Am I right?" And they would say, "Yeah, you're right." "OK, well good. I can see that you might be a little nervous and maybe a little anxious and if you are, that's perfectly OK. Most of my customers are. This is probably a new experience for you, but I've been handling claims for four maybe five years now and I've got a pretty good handle on what it's going to take to make sure this goes smoothly. I don't have a crystal ball and I can't promise the world. But

I will tell you this: I am going to do everything I can to make sure this claim does go smoothly because I understand how important this is to you, especially as my customer. Does that sound good?" After he finished this little speech, guess what people would say: "Yeah, that sounds great." And what did they almost always forget? All of the questions piled up. So, with Carl as the adjuster and Teresa as the customer, Teresa is going to ask Carl some questions. We are at the end of the conversation and she's already asked questions. We'll start with that. She's already asked him the nervous, anxious questions we tend to get. What about this? How come this? Why is that? Instead of wearing her out with a bunch of answers, Carl is going to use his newfound skills to see if he can't give her some reassurance, which by the way, is probably what she wanted anyway.

Adjuster (Carl Van): "Alright Teresa, I can tell it is very important to you that this claim goes smoothly. Am I right?"

Customer (Teresa Headrick): "Yes, you are."

Adjuster: "OK, you know, you might be a little nervous, maybe a little anxious, and if you are, it's perfectly OK. A lot of my customers are. I know this is kind of new for you, maybe even a little scary, but I've been handling claims for a number of years now and I've got a pretty good handle on what it's going to take to make sure your claims goes smoothly. I can't promise the world, but I can tell you this. I am going to do everything I can to make sure that this claim does go smoothly because I appreciate how important it is to you. Does that sound OK?"

Customer: "It does."

Adjuster: "Alright, great."

So, will this work? Maybe it will and maybe it won't. Our guess is, though, it's probably going to work a lot better than just wearing her out with all of the answers to all of the questions she has. In claims, we have a wonderful opportunity to gain trust and credibility by demonstrating we understand where our customers are coming from. Like we said before, our customers are a little bit different. They had a bad experience. They didn't want it, they didn't ask for it, and they don't like it. Sometimes they need some special attention from us.

Carl has had people ask him, "Would you write this out so we could read it to customers?" There's no way. If Carl did that, guess what some people would do? They'd read it to the customer. That's not the point. The point is you are skilled enough, talented enough, and professional enough in your job to be able to relate to the customer. "I understand this is important. I've got some experience and some training and some knowledge I'm going to use to help you." Do you have that ability? Well, we are going to find out because we're going to give you a chance to practice right now.

We are going to do the exercise, but before we do, let's recap. Step number one in overcoming the question after question cycle is *acknowledge*. Acknowledge you understand where the other person is coming from, that this is important. Number two is *empathy*. "You might be nervous; you might be anxious." Keep it casual. Step number three is *permission*. "If you are nervous and anxious, it's perfectly OK." Let them know the way they are feeling is fine. Number four is *experience*. Make a modest statement about your level of experience. Number five, *promise* you are going to do whatever it takes to make sure the claim goes smoothly. What we want you to do now is see if you can try these five steps. It's OK to look at your notes. It's OK if you don't get it perfectly. We are just practicing right now. Do your best as you practice the five steps.

How did you do, OK? It's alright if you didn't do great. We are going to practice this. Before we continue, we want to make a point about a couple of things. The first one: acknowledge. Carl has had someone say to him, "Well Carl, if you say this to a customer, 'I understand this claim is important to you,' they're going to say 'well, of course it is. What are you, an idiot?'" You have to understand who you are talking to. You're talking to someone who's *so* nervous and anxious, they're actually asking you question after question after question. This person is not going to be insulted by a statement like "I understand this is important." By the way, who are you going to use this with? Your individual customers, maybe the insured or claimant, people who have suffered a loss. Are you going to use this with vendors or attorneys or anybody outside? Are you going to call up a body shop and say, "Hey, I know you guys have to pull that frame today. I know you might be a little nervous and anxious." No. You are going to use this with customers who are demonstrating that they are nervous and anxious.

For empathy, you don't have to go overboard. You don't have to say, "Oh, you poor person, we're going to pick up the poor shattered pieces of your crumbled life. We have a hotline number waiting for you if you might need it anytime." We're not going to go overboard. A very casual statement is sufficient. "I know, you might be nervous and anxious." You don't have to say, "I know you are upset." Some people might say, "I'm not upset!" Just say, "I know you might be nervous and anxious." Don't pin them down. Don't make them admit it. "I know you're nervous and anxious." Keep it casual and give them a backdoor out. "You might be a little nervous and anxious, and if you are, it's certainly OK."

AWESOME CLAIMS CUSTOMER SERVICE

As far as experience goes, if you have a lot of experience that is great. Just don't brag like we mentioned before. It really doesn't add credibility. But what if you have hardly any experience? Well, if you were to say to a customer, "I know you might be a little nervous, maybe a little anxious, but I've been handling claims for five days now," you might not get the level of trust you are looking for. But Carl has actually heard people say something along the lines of, "you know what, I know you might be a little nervous, maybe a little anxious, and this is new for you. But you know what, this is my job, this is what I do." There. You don't even have to say how long you have been doing it. Just something to let them know this is your profession and you take it seriously.

The fifth step is promise. Can you promise that everything is going to go OK? No. What can you promise? You can promise that you are going to do everything you can to make sure that it does. You know what your job is in claims? Your job is to do whatever it takes to make sure that this claim goes smoothly. We're in the customer service business. You know what you just promised to do? Your job-this is what you do for a living. You make sure that claims go smoothly. There isn't anything that you could possibly do that isn't your job that's related to this issue. We have a suggestion: Don't do this until you believe it. We would not make this promise. If one of us was a claims representative practicing these skills right now, go through all four, do your best, but until you believe your job is to do whatever it takes to make sure the claim goes smoothly, then we would recommend that you don't say it. Don't take that fifth step until you believe it. Wait until you believe it to give it a try. As we mentioned, we're going to practice this again. Before we do, we've got something we want to share with you.

We want to tell you about a customer service class Carl was in. They had students enter the classroom one at a time about five minutes apart, and Carl was the fifth person. So, Carl comes walking into the room. The other four guys who were there before him are in the corner smiling at Carl, so he knows he's in for something. They say, "Carl, here's a jar of jelly beans. There's your customer, go satisfy your customer."

So, Carl walks over to the person who's supposed to be the customer and he says, "Yeah, how can I help you?" and they say, "Well, I would like a jelly bean please." "Oh, OK." Carl takes out a jelly bean and replies, "There you go." "Anything else I can do for you?" "Yeah, I'd like another jelly bean please." "No problem," and he takes out another jelly bean. "There you go." "Is there anything else I can do for you? Anything at all?" "Yeah, another jelly bean would be great." "Alright, here you go. Here's another jelly bean." How many times did this go on, do you think, before Carl finally asked a question?

AWESOME CLAIMS CUSTOMER SERVICE

What question do you think Carl should ask? "How many jelly beans do you want? You know I don't have all day." Well, when Carl finally got bored after about five or six, he finally said, "Well, how many jelly beans do you want?" Notice— not when he realized his customer needed something more than he was giving him—no, no, no when *Carl* got bored he finally said, "Well, how many jelly beans do you want?" They said, "All of them." "Oh, here you go." "OK, Carl," he was told, "You're done. Go over there with the other four guys." So, Carl walked over to those four guys and sat down and said, "Well, how many did you guys take?" "Well, not as many as you Carl, but try to pay attention."

Then something interesting happened. While Carl was watching, another person walked into the room. At this point, it was person number seven. This person walked in and you know how many times it took this person? It took him twenty-two times. That's no lie. Carl and the others were over in the corner with tears coming out of their eyes trying not to laugh. They figured they were going to find out how many jelly beans there were in the jar. But after about five or six, he gets a little bored too and he says, "You know, why don't you just tell me straight out, (like the customer has been lying to him), what is it that you want?" "I want another jelly bean." "Oh, here you go." After about eleven, he gets a little annoyed and says, "You know, I'm trying to help you, and you are not being very cooperative here. You need to tell me what you want." "I want another jelly bean." He's getting irritated. After about eighteen, he starts getting a little rude. He says, "You know what, either you're too stupid to understand or you don't want to understand, I'm trying to help you but you have to tell me, what do you want." "I want another jelly bean." "Ahh, this is ridiculous." Finally, finally, finally, after twenty-two times, he doesn't lose his cool completely, but he gets irritated and he says, "You know what, this conversation is over. You know what you are, you're one of those customers, no matter what I do, it's not going to be good enough for you. So, you know what, this conversation is over unless you want to tell me how many damn jelly beans you want" and the customer says, "All of them." "Oh, why didn't you just say so? Oh, these stupid customers. I can't believe it; why don't they just tell you what they want?" He comes walking over to the rest of the group and they are moving away, you know, because he's pretty upset. The very next person walked into the room and something quite different happened with this person.

This person walks in, they give him a jar of jelly beans and he walks over to the customer and says, "Yeah, how can I help you?" And the customer says, "I'd like a jelly bean please." He says, "Sure, how many would you like?" The customer says, "All of them." "Here you go." You're done. This whole exercise was meant to do two things. The first one is to find out how long it's going to take you before it dawns on you that your customer needs something more than you are giving them. Is it one question? Is it six questions? Is it twenty-two questions? When does it finally hit you that your customer needs something more than you are giving them? And you know what the second one was? The customer is going to get all the jelly beans anyway. The only question for you is which process do you want to take? The customer is going to drag credibility, they are going to drag trust out of you, question by question, demand after demand, challenge after challenge. Or you can just *hand* it to them. Either way works just fine.

Yes, it's time to practice it again. If you can, have a little fun with this. It's OK if it doesn't go perfectly. In claims we have the opportunity to let customers know they can trust us. We can gain credibility. We have it at our fingertips. All we need to do is reach out and get it. In this case, what we want you to do is see if you can just practice the five steps. They don't have to be in order. Just do the very best you can.

Did you do well? It's alright if it doesn't go perfectly. Things of value take time and take some practice. Here's a suggestion for you: The next time you have a nervous and anxious customer, just start with one. Don't try all five. If you try to throw in all five steps the very first time, you know what's going to happen? You're going to say something that's going to feel stupid, you're not going to do it ever again and it's going to get tossed by the wayside. Here's a suggestion: Just use the first step. If you feel that someone's very nervous and anxious, just say something along the lines of, "You know what, I can tell this is really important to you. Am I right?" And they'll say, "Yeah, yeah you're right." Then just forget it. After that, just handle the claim like you normally would. Do that about five or six or seven times and what happens? You start to get into the habit. You start getting positive reinforcement that what you said is being well taken and you're going to feel comfortable with what you are saying. Then, when you are nice and comfortable with that, then throw in, "You might be nervous and anxious and if you are, it's OK." Do all of that about six, seven, or eight times and then start throwing in some experience. And then finally, only after all four steps seem nice and comfortable to you, throw in the fifth step, "I'm going to do everything I can to make sure this process goes smoothly." Wait until all four steps are nice and comfortable before throwing in the fifth one because it's the most powerful and it has to be the most believed. Well, now we are going to move on to a new section and we hope you're looking forward to this one.

CHAPTER 10

The Five Standards for Great Claims Customer Service

Our next section has to do with the five standards for great claims customer service. We have already talked about the five standards for great customer service companies. The five standards for great claims customer service are more specific to claims.

Clear and Consistent Communication

The first one is clear and consistent communication. Our customers are entitled to have the same story told to them, so they understand. They are entitled to understand the entire process. Nail down questions are a perfect example of a time where we improve consistent communication and make it clear because people now are listening while we're talking and remembering what we're saying.

Empathy

The second standard is empathy. This is a very important standard for us in claims. We've mentioned before, our customers have had something bad happen to them. And sometimes, they need a little bit of extra empathy. Sometimes, we're disappointed at the level of empathy we show our customers. The longer you've been in this business, well, it's easy to have that level of empathy go down because, well, you've heard it all. But to a customer, sometimes right now in their life, this is the worst thing that has happened to them. And they deserve a level of empathy no matter how big or small the claim is. In our training classes, Carl will ask his students, "When do you provide empathy?" and sometimes people say, "Well, when there's blood, if there's a child that's been injured, if it's a total loss, something serious." And they'll always relate to, "when it's serious." Well, we tend to empathize with our customers when, if we were in their place, it would rattle us. But what happens the longer you've been in this business? Well, that bar starts to rise. And you know what, after a while, there are not too many things that you can hear that people go through that would really shake us up. But you know what, even to a guy whose fender got scratched, this is still a guy who has to pay five hundred dollars maybe for his deductible who doesn't have it this month. This is still someone who wanted to buy a washing machine now and can't. This can still be a traumatic and unfamiliar event to this person and a level of empathy to that person is appropriate in our business.

We want to give you a quick example of a situation involving empathy. Tell us what you think. Carl was monitoring phone calls at this one company and they didn't really have a very good phone system. So, he decided to sit down next to people and listen to what they were doing. Carl sat down next to a loss report taker and she was trying to help a customer who had just called in right after an accident. And so, she was asking the customer questions like, "Ma'am, do you know where your car is?" "Yes, I know where my car is, what a dumb question. It's right out in front, it's smashed, it's wrecked, for crying out loud." "Alright, ma'am, OK. Are you injured?" "Yes, I've got a big cut down my arm, it's bleeding, I'm practically dying right now." "Alright ma'am, OK." "How long is this going to take, what's going on there?" The loss report taker was doing her best trying to answer the questions and finally at the end of the conversation she says, "OK, ma'am, I'm going to go ahead and have someone call you." "Well, that will be a big relief, if you can do that, it would be nice to have somebody finally help me." "OK, we will." She hangs up, turns to Carl, and says, "Man, what was her problem?" Like, what kind of crazy person is this? You know what's wrong with this person? Did she get a bad night's sleep? You know what's wrong? Well, Carl knows what was wrong. She had been in an auto accident. She's scared out of her mind, for crying out loud. That loss report taker, Carl didn't blame her for her reaction. She had been around for a long time and something as simple as a little auto accident maybe in her mind shouldn't have gotten the customer so upset and shouldn't have gotten the customer yelling at her. "Why is she yelling at me?" Well, you know what, that's what customers do. For us to have a level of empathy, any time anything happens, in claims, is important. Why? Because it's our job. This is what we do. We help people when something bad has happened to them. Keep that in mind.

Excellent Follow-up and Follow-through

The third standard is excellent follow-up and follow-through. You know, as an industry, we are pretty good at following through on our promises, when we know we've made them. Many times, we don't know we've made them. Going back to the setting expectations issue, when you tell a customer something like, "Alright, as soon as I hear from that person, I'll call you," you've set an expectation. You have made a promise. You just don't know it. When we say things like, "As soon as I get this, I'll send that to you, as soon as I find this out, I'll call you," we're setting expectations in their mind without even knowing it. And by the way, every expectation that you set is a promise they think you've made to them. So, we're very good at keeping our promises when we know we've made them. What we must start doing is a better job of knowing when we have made them. So, instead of saying, "I'll call you as soon as I get this report," you might want to say, "You know what, I'll call you as soon as I get this report. It should be by Friday." And then of course, if you don't get it by Friday, you know you still need to call that person. So, all of that has to do with the way people *feel* they are being treated. Many people leave an insurance company after a claim, up to seventy five percent, because of the way they *feel* they are being treated. One of the most important issues people refer to when they talk about the way they feel they are being treated is whether or not we kept our promise. They feel they have been lied to, sometimes, inadvertently, simply because we didn't set an expectation. So, we're very good in our follow through, we're very good at keeping our promises, but we've got to realize when we've made them and be clear on that issue.

AWESOME CLAIMS CUSTOMER SERVICE

Fair and Accurate Settlements

Our fourth standard for outstanding claims customer service is fair and accurate settlements. Once again here, we do a very good job of being fair. Our figures are fair, and we know it. Unfortunately, sometimes the way we give that information and try to convince people of that, they don't always feel they've been treated fairly. You might be in worker's comp, you might be in commercial, you might be in homeowner's, auto, it doesn't matter. Overall, as an industry, we're pretty fair and accurate. But if our customers don't feel that way, what good is it? We talked about the fact that the way people feel is why they're leaving us in our business. And you know what, as far as our settlements go, if we're fair, that's good. But if our customers feel we're not being fair, that's not good. What do we mean? We'll explain.

Being fair has to do with letting people know we understand where they are coming from. We talked before about the claims hammer. Sometimes we use it to get people to cooperate. "If you don't do this, (Bam) this is what is going to happen." Well, sometimes that claims hammer comes out in our settlements. We're being fair but the way we're explaining that to our customer, "If you don't take this amount of money, you're going to have to pay storage," (Bam), "If you don't take this, you're going to have to make your car payments," (Bam), whatever it is, sometimes the way we explain it to our customers can sound like a threat and an ultimatum and then they don't feel like they're being treated fairly. What is the best way to let someone know that you are going to treat them fairly? By repeating back to them why they feel that way. Why they feel the value of the claim is that. Whatever it is, if we can acknowledge their point of view, often, they will feel that they were treated fairly. Even if they don't get what they want, at least if they are being heard, they'll feel that they were treated fairly. That's a big piece.

Prompt and Final Resolution

And our fifth and final standard, which you've probably heard if you've ever heard anybody talk about survey results from customers, is prompt and final resolution. You know what, people want to have their claim over with. They don't want it dragged out. They want it handled quickly, promptly, and fairly, and have it done with. This is one of our key elements in claims. Sometimes it doesn't always happen and sometimes things take a long time. That's where setting expectations is key. Letting somebody know what to expect, even if it's going to take a long time, can still make them feel that it was handled promptly. So, these are our five standards. Let's review.

AWESOME CLAIMS CUSTOMER SERVICE

The five standards for great claims customer service are clear and consistent communication, empathy, excellent follow-up and follow-through, fair and accurate settlements, and prompt and final resolution.

Allow us to just mention one little thing at the end of this. Let's say there is a claims person, and let's say this person reports to Carl and Carl is the supervisor. Carl walks up to this employee and says, "You know what, you're going to be getting a call in a few minutes and this is going to be the most important customer you ever deal with. I mean in your entire career here at this company, you will never deal with a more important customer than this person. So, heads up." That will probably scare the heck out of that person, right? But we want to make a point. Would you see a change in this person? The employee, if we said this to him, would you see a change? Would you see this person pay attention more? If the customer was rattling on about something, they might focus on what the customer was saying? If this employee had to make a phone call, even if they didn't perceive it was their job, but it would make the claims process go smoother, would they do it? You bet. As a matter of fact, you would see a lot of change in this particular employee. Here's what we want you to think about. First of all, any change that you could imagine that you would see in this employee, you are actually imagining what you would change for yourself. That's number one. And number two, it points out all the areas of opportunity, because anything that you could imagine this person changing is probably your opportunity for improvement either for yourself or your company. These are all things that you could do if you wanted to, you just don't want to. And the reason you don't want to is very fair. Because it would take too much time. Ahh... This again is where the time management experts would have to step in and say, "Well, no, not really. See, because every single thing that you would change, everything you would do, would ultimately save you time."

You see, the extra time you might provide giving empathy, is only going to increase that person's trust in you. That phone call you might make, even though you normally wouldn't, you might make it because it's going to make the claims process go smoothly, somehow, someway, and make it easier for someone else down the line. Virtually everything that you would do, right now in this stage, for that particular customer, will somehow, someway, ultimately save you, or your claims operation, time. The idea that providing outstanding customer service takes more time is a complete myth. It's not even true. If you want to be a great claims professional, providing outstanding customer service, you're going to find two things. Your job becomes easier and you save yourself some time.

CHAPTER 11

Active Listening

Our next section has to do with active listening. We said it would make our jobs easier if customers would just listen. And we talked about a way to get that to happen. You know what would also make our jobs much easier? If we would listen a little bit better, ourselves. We mentioned before that when Carl monitors phone calls, customers are telling us exactly what they want. We are just not listening. If we apply just a couple active listening skills, we'll make our job much easier and improve customer service along the way.

In claims, our customers do three basic things when we're talking to them: The first is they ask questions; the next is they offer objections; and the third is they make statements. Now, if you're not using your active listening skills, you might get confused about which of these is happening. We're pretty good at knowing when someone asks a question. But sometimes, if someone makes a snide comment when they're asking a question, like, "Oh, thanks for calling, *finally*, is that the best you can do?" they may not be really asking that question. Or, Carl even heard one recently where a customer actually said to a claims person, "What are you guys there, a bunch of morons?" and the claims person said, "Well, no, we're not morons; we've all graduated from college and... blah blah blah blah." We don't think the customer was really asking that question. But overall, we're pretty good at knowing when someone asks us questions. It's when they make statements and offer objections, that sometimes we get confused, and it can be dangerous for the claims professional.

When a claims person becomes confused between a customer's statement and a customer's objection, it's usually simply because we don't understand the difference between making a statement and offering an objection from the customer's point of view. If a customer were to say to you, "You know what, I didn't get payment nearly as soon as I thought I should have," this person isn't really offering an objection. And by the way, when someone offers an objection, you need to get involved. If they're just making a statement, they're just looking for a reaction, kind of like a snide comment. So when the customer says, "I didn't get payment as soon as I thought I should have," our response probably should be, "You know what, if you didn't get it as soon as you thought you were going to, I do apologize. We understand paying promptly is important and I am sorry it didn't happen." Just a nice simple reaction to the statement. But if this person says, "Well I didn't get my payment as soon as I thought I should have and I want to talk to a manager," that's an objection and that's something you need to get involved in. How do you tell the difference? It's pretty simple.

If a customer implies that they are going to take some future action, they are going to be doing something because of this issue, you pretty much need to get involved and help solve the problem. Short of that, your best response is to simply apologize for the situation and move on. That's the difference between an objection which requires your involvement and a statement, which simply requires your acknowledgement. If they say, "Your person wasn't out to my loss as soon as they should have been," they're just making a statement. Apologize. "If our person wasn't out as soon as you thought they should have been, I do apologize. We understand that this is important." If they say something like, "Well, your guy wasn't out as soon as I thought he should be and maybe I need to look for a new insurance company," that's an objection. How do you tell the difference? In the second instance, the customer implied that they were going to take some action. If they don't actually say something like, "Maybe I should speak to a manager," or "Maybe I should look for a new insurance company," or "Maybe I should talk to my agent," if they don't actually say something that they are going to do, it's probably just a statement. And we'll show you how we get involved in an argument because we don't understand that difference.

When a person says something like, "That guy you sent out didn't call me as soon as he should have, and you respond with, "When did he say he was going to call?", notice what is happening. You're actually getting involved in the issue when all the customer is looking for is a reaction. Guess what? No matter what you say and how this goes back and forth, this can't end well because you're drawing out the fact that the customer is disappointed. You really don't need to try to solve the problem. What's your best reaction? "If they weren't out as soon as they should have been, if they didn't call when you thought they should have, (whatever it is), I'm sorry about that. We understand this is important. We apologize it didn't happen." This is what the person is looking for. You can make your job much easier and improve customer service by giving the customer what they want: a reaction.

Active listening also means knowing the difference between what people want to hear and what they expect to hear. You know, as a claims professional, many times, customers just hear what they want to hear. We know that. We hear that all the time from claims people. Customers just hear what they want to hear. It might be true in many cases. But it's also true that people hear what they expect to hear. As a matter of fact, there is something called the *law of expectations*. The law of expectations says that you will hear what you expect to hear and you will see what you expect to see and that truth is so strong, it can override what you hear versus what the person really said and what you see versus what's actually in front of you. We know that's hard to believe. We are going to give you an exercise to try to make that point. But the reason we're bringing this up is because in claims, we have a very high expectation of what we think people are about to say, don't we?

As a matter of fact, we could even finish our customer's sentences sometimes, can't we? We know we're sitting there talking to a customer, we're trying to listen, but we're just waiting for them to finish what they are saying so we can now, of course, jump in with, "Yes, but, you know... yes but..." Sometimes that might be complaining about something. Sometimes we know they are going to demand something. We're just waiting for them to finish so we can now tell them what we have to tell them. If

AWESOME CLAIMS CUSTOMER SERVICE

we have a very high expectation of what a customer's going to say, there's a good chance we're hearing what we're expecting, even if it's not what they are actually saying. When Carl monitors phone calls, this happens very frequently. A claims professional will respond to a customer with what they think they heard because they had a very specific expectation—even though that's not exactly what the customer said.

Alright, let's get started. We're going to give you a sentence then give you a task that might be a challenge for you. Now, the very first challenge we give you is going to be so basic, so easy, there's no way you could get it wrong. Then we're going to make it more and more complicated and see if a difference exists between what you think you see and what is actually there.

The sentence below doesn't really mean anything; don't try to find any intrinsic value. We know it's kind of a tongue twister. Read it out loud then count the number of "F's" you see.

Frequently files of Fred's are the first of all of the fat files to go to litigation.

What did you come up with? Six? Seven? Eight? Maybe nine? There's a good chance that everyone is going to come up with a different answer. When we do this exercise in class, we like to use it to show people that everybody sees things differently. We come up with different answers all the time. Some people will say six while others may say seven, eight, or nine. The point is that people can look at the same thing and see different things. Why? Believe it or not, it's because of the law of expectations, which we will demonstrate shortly. The point is that we can see things differently if we have different expectations and, believe it or not, we led you down this path. Before we get to the right answer, try it just one more time. Take a good look at the sentence again. Tell us how many "F's" you think there are.

Frequently files of Fred's are the first of all of the fat files to go to litigation.

Did you get a different number this time? Some people probably did. If you got six, seven or eight, we have bad news for you. The answer is nine. Some of you might have gotten it. Some of you are still convinced it's seven, eight, or who knows. We'll go through it together, but we want to make a point. If you didn't see nine, it's because you fell into the trap of the law of expectations. You see, we tend to read phonetically and when we read something out loud, the words *frequently*, *files*, and *Fred*, sound like an "F," but when we get to the word *of*, well that kind of sounds like a "V." When you read this out loud, *frequently files of Fred's*, what you heard phonetically actually planted a seed in your mind where there are and aren't "F's." And some of us, even though we looked at the word *of*, even though our eye made contact with the letter "F," we didn't actually see it because our expectation is it's not there.

Let us go through this right now. *F*requently *f*iles *of F*red's are the *f*irst *of* all *of* the *f*at *f*iles to go to litigation. Well, did you finally get nine? Don't feel bad if you didn't. It's very common. People can stare at this for half an hour and sometimes not get it because their expectation is very high. Again, the law of expectation says you will hear what you expect to hear and see what you expect to see, and that truth is so strong it can override what you actually see in front of you and what you actually think you hear. The reason this is so important in claims is because we have a very high expectation of what we think customers are saying or complaining about.

If we want to do an outstanding job of listening to our customers, we have to drop any expectation of what we think the customer is going to say. That's not easy when you've been doing this job for a long time. When you're at the point you can already finish customers' sentences, there's a good chance you're hearing what you expect to hear. So how do we stop having these types of expectations? Well, it's not easy, but it's not impossible. We're going to get into an exercise and a demonstration to help you.

Before we get started, we'll give you a very clear example. Carl heard a conversation, in this case it was a worker's comp adjuster, talking to a customer and explaining the medical authorization form. About halfway through the conversation, the customer says, "Well, I don't understand why I have to sign that dumb form," and the adjuster responds with, "Well, you have to sign it because of this and that etc." The customer continued with, "Well, I don't understand why I have to sign that stupid form" and the adjuster was getting a little irritated, and repeated, "Well, we've got to have it. It's not stupid and blah, blah, blah..." and they went back and forth. The adjuster actually got irritated with this customer and took it out on him. Well, when Carl went to this claims adjuster, he said, "Why did that upset you so much?" and the adjuster said, "Well, because the customer was calling me dumb. They called me stupid." Carl said, "No, they weren't calling you stupid. They were calling the form stupid." "No, they were calling me stupid" he insisted. "No, they called the form stupid," Carl persisted. "Do you want to hear the tape?" Carl had to play the tape back for this worker's comp person. Why? Because what that person actually *heard* was, "You're stupid." What the customer *said* was, "the form is stupid." This is a good example of the times we hear things because we expect to hear them.

AWESOME CLAIMS CUSTOMER SERVICE

The following dialog is a role play. What do you think this customer is angry about? Read it and see if you can tell.

Adjuster (Dave): "Hello, this is Dave from International Insurance...

Customer (Ms. Scortino): "Hi, I'm calling about my check?"

Adjuster: ...ah, your check, with whom am I speaking please?"

Customer: "Evelyn Scortino, I'm just calling to find out when I can expect it."

Adjuster: "Ah, Ms. Scortino, yeah, OK, what is your claim..."

Customer: "Yeah, 123456."

Adjuster: ...number please? Yeah, OK, great, can I put you..."

Customer: "Yeah, go ahead, put me on hold."

Adjuster: "...on hold just a minute? Yes, Ms. Scortino, I see here on the system that your check was mailed out yester...

Customer: "OK, great thanks, bye bye."

Adjuster: "...day. Ah.... goodbye."

So, what do you think? What was the customer angry about? Was she angry about the fact that she didn't get her check? Was she angry about the fact that things were late? What do you think? Maybe some of you say, well, she wasn't really angry, not as far as I could tell. And you'd be right. In this case, this is what we call an assertive/demanding customer. Not angry, but assertive/demanding. How do you know? Well, customers like this don't even let you finish saying, *hello* before they tell you what they want. They say, "uh huh, uh huh," sometimes to get you to talk faster. And as soon as you say anything that even resembles an answer, they say, OK, goodbye. See, they think very quickly, and they think this conversation is over. So, in this case, this customer isn't angry, just assertive/demanding. But something did happen that's going to make her angry. Did you catch that?

Here is a question for you: What expectation does this customer have now about when she's going to get a check? We said it went out yesterday. Any reasonable person would think it's going to be there in a few days, right? Well, we can tell you one thing about assertive/demanding people. They shorten the time frame on anything you give them. If you tell an assertive/demanding person, "We'll be there between two and four," they'll only hear what? Two. If you say something will take two to three days, often they'll just hear two. If you tell an assertive/demanding person the check went out yesterday, when are they going to expect that check? Today, that's right. And when they go out today and look into that mailbox, and the check is not there, now they are calling you back. And guess what? Now they *are* angry. Why? Because they feel they have been lied to. Had we told them the truth; their check would be there. But since it wasn't, guess what, they feel they got lied to. We don't want this to happen to assertive/demanding customers. They are good customers. What we have to do is make sure we set expectations at all times. We'll explain that.

Given what the adjuster told our customer here, there's no chance she's going to wait three or four days for this check. Here's a suggestion: With assertive/demanding people, always set a very clear and specific time frame. They shorten the time frame on anything you give them. If you tell them the check went out yesterday, you should have it in a couple of days, well, to them, yesterday was one, today must be two. And again, they are expecting their check today. You want to say something very specific. The check went out yesterday, it takes two or three days for the mail, today is Tuesday, you should definitely have it by Friday. And actually, say the word *Friday*. See, to an assertive/demanding person, you have to give them a very clear expectation. Now Carl has had some people say, "They'll still call you on Wednesday." Oh no they won't. Assertive/demanding people always want things immediately, but they are very respectful of deadlines. If you tell this person, "It will be there on Friday," they will not call you on Wednesday. They will not call you on Thursday. On Friday, two feet after the postman leaves their mailbox, if that check is not there, believe us, they're on the phone to you. They will wait for a clear expectation if you give them one.

When did it seem like that customer was angry? Well, assertive/demanding people, as we mentioned previously, sometimes interrupt. Is it rude, to interrupt? Perhaps but to an assertive/demanding person, interrupting is perfectly reasonable. You see, they are very busy; they have a lot to do. For them to wait for you to finish "Hello, my name is Carl Van, at the insurance company, how may I help you?" is almost painful. They are extremely fast thinkers. They are not into the social side of business. They just want their check. That's all they want. Waiting for you to finish sentences can sometimes be difficult, and you say, well, that's rude. Yes, OK, fine, that's rude *to you*, but to an assertive/demanding person, it really isn't rude behavior. So, how do you solve this problem? Well, as we mentioned before, you can keep on talking. Believe it or not, an assertive/demanding person won't find your behavior rude. Here's what's rude: letting them off the phone with a false expectation.

Here's a suggestion for how to handle an assertive/demanding person in this situation. Remember, assertive/demanding people sometimes talk when you're talking which means you can talk when they're talking. This isn't rude behavior to them. What's rude? False expectations are rude. So, as strange as it seems, here's the solution for how to answer that particular problem. You're talking to an assertive/demanding person and they're saying, "I want my check," and you say, "Well, what is your claim number?" don't be surprised if they interrupt you. "What is your claim num..." "one, two, three, four, five, six." "Can I put you on ho..." "Yes, you can put me on hold." They know what you are going to say. You come back and say, "Alright, well, let's see the check went out yester..." "OK, thanks, goodbye." You just keep talking. "And let's see, since it went out yesterday, it takes two to three days for the ma..." "OK, thanks, goodbye." "You should get it on Friday and if you don't get it on Friday, give me a ca..." "OK, thanks, goodbye." "OK, goodbye. Have a nice day." Something along those lines. Believe it or not, to an assertive/demanding person, this is a perfectly cordial conversation.

Believe it or not, you have 100 percent control over this conversation. Why? Because you can keep talking and make sure that customer doesn't hang up until you say what you want to say. This isn't rude behavior. Remember what we said? When an assertive/demanding person thinks they hear the answer, "The check went out yesterday," they want to leave. "OK, goodbye." They are trying to get you to say goodbye by saying goodbye to you. Why are they trying to get you to say goodbye? So, they can hang up. Believe it or not, they won't hang up until you say goodbye. Do you know why? Because for them to hang up before you say goodbye, well, that would be rude. They don't want to be rude; they are trying to be polite.

Even if you feel it's rude, they are not trying to be rude. What you want to do is make sure you set that expectation. Now, we have a role play here. The adjuster is going to take another shot at it and do his best. Tell us what you think.

Adjuster (Dave): "Hello, this is Dave..."

Customer (Ms. Scortino): "Hi, I'm calling about my check?"

Adjuster: "ah your check, who am I speaking with...?"

AWESOME CLAIMS CUSTOMER SERVICE

Customer: "Yeah, I'm just calling to find out when I can expect my check."

Adjuster: "...please?"

Customer: "This is Evelyn Scortino."

Adjuster: "Ah, Ms. Scor..."

Customer: "Yes."

Adjuster: "...Tino, great, what is your claim..."

Customer: "Yes, it's 123456."

Adjuster: "...number please? Ah, OK, great let me put you on..."

Customer: "OK, go ahead, put me on hold."

Adjuster: "...hold for just a minute. Ah, yes, Ms. Scor..."

Customer: "Yes, I'm here."

Adjuster: "...tino, OK, looking at the screen, it appears your check was mailed out..."

Customer: "Yeah."

Adjuster: "...yester..."

Customer: "OK, great, thank you, bye bye."

Adjuster: "...day, ah, hold on just a moment Ms. Scortino, yeah, these things obviously take a few days to get through the post..."

Customer: "OK."

Adjuster: "ah, it was mailed yesterday on Monday, you should expect to get that on Fri..."

Customer: "Alright, thank you, bye bye."

Adjuster: "...day. One more thing too, if you don't get it by Friday, please, give me a call, and we'll look ..."

Customer: "Ok, thanks, bye bye."

Adjuster: "... into it. Alright, goodbye."

How did he do? Maybe not perfect. There is no perfect solution in this case. We'll tell you one thing, though, he did very well. He didn't let this customer off the phone with a false expectation. One thing you don't want to do with assertive/demanding people is assume they are angry. That's one of the worst things you can do. Recently, Carl heard a good adjuster talking to an assertive/demanding person and he said, "Well, sir, if you will just stay calm." You know what happens when you tell an assertive/demanding person to stay calm? They get angry. Why? Because they are always being confused with people who are angry. And they are not angry, just assertive/demanding. They are not being rude. They're not trying to be anyway. That's important, because you're going to need patience in dealing with an assertive/demanding person, because if you feel someone's being rude to you, what might you do back? You might be rude back. So, to know that someone is not trying to be rude is a real key element with the assertive/demanding person.

So, if you want to make your job easier and improve customer service, be sure to treat assertive/demanding people how they like to be treated. Remember, the assertive/demanding person is quick to show authority and demand action, and they tend to get to the point immediately.

Listed below are a few tips for dealing with the assertive/demanding person:

1. Listen, so you will be able to understand their problems or concerns.

2. Match some of the customer's assertiveness when appropriate.

3. Use closed end questions to help control the conversation.

4. Be friendly but specific and direct in your statements.

CHAPTER 12

Dealing with the Angry Customer

Now it's time to talk about angry customers—not just assertive/demanding, but angry. And we get angry customers. We want to talk about a five-step process that can help in dealing with angry customers. Not every customer is going to fit into the categories that will be helped by this process, but a large majority will. Would you agree that sometimes the hardest part in dealing with angry customers is to just calm them down long enough so that we can help them? We said it would make our job easier if people were calm and patient. Well, what is it that we can do that can make someone calm down? Do we do anything at all? Well sometimes

AWESOME CLAIMS CUSTOMER SERVICE

we try to help them. We try to solve their problem but that may not calm them down. One of the biggest keys to improving customer service, and dealing with the angry person, is to do something which can calm them down long enough so that we can help them and that's one of the steps of this five step process.

Remember that question we asked, "Why do we get fifty phone calls?" Well, here's a perfect example we want to share with you of something Carl actually heard on why we get too many phone calls. In this case, we didn't have a good process on how to deal with an angry customer. An adjuster got a call from somebody who was upset about something that happened at the body shop. The customer called up and said, "I am so upset with you guys." And the adjuster asked, "What happened?" "Well, you guys told the body shop to put the wrong parts on my car. What are you guys, a bunch of idiots?" "Oh, I don't know why we would do that. That doesn't sound like something we would do. Let me go ahead and call the body shop and I'll call you right back." So, let us ask you a question: What's the customer's expectation? Yes, that he will be called right back. Well the adjuster calls the body shop, he needs to talk to Stan, so he asks for Stan and guess what? Stan's out to lunch. So, he says, "Well, have Stan call me as soon as he comes back." What does the adjuster have to do now? He's got to call the customer back and say, "Sorry, I've got to talk to

Stan. I'll call you back later." But guess what, Stan does call. The adjuster is on the phone. The call rolls into his voice mail. He calls Stan back and guess what, Stan's out there pulling a frame right now, he promises he'll get back to you. So, guess what, Stan finally does call and finally gets a hold of the adjuster. How many phone calls are we up to already?

So, after a couple of phone calls back and forth to the body shop and of course, back and forth to the customer, we've now made a lot of phone calls, right? The adjuster finally gets a hold of Stan and he says, "Stan, what's going on?" Stan says, "What do you mean?" "Well my customer says that you guys put the wrong parts on his car." And Stan says, "No, they're the right parts. It looks beautiful." "Well, the customer said the wrong parts were on the car." "No, they're perfect, it's a work of art!" And the adjuster says, "Well, why is the customer saying this?" and Stan says, "I don't know, why don't you ask him?" Think about this. We've now made five, six, seven, phone calls, who knows, and the adjuster at this point doesn't really understand the issue. Why? Because he's confused an assertive/demanding person with an angry person. Here's what we mean.

See, the funny thing about it is we always think assertive/demanding people are angry, and we always think angry people are in a hurry. This guy is not

AWESOME CLAIMS CUSTOMER SERVICE

in a hurry, he's just upset. And what happened was the claims adjuster was in such a hurry to get off the phone, he didn't follow the five steps that can really help calm someone down long enough to help them. Well, here's what happened. When the adjuster finally did call the customer back, he said, "You know what sir, can you tell me what you mean when you say the body shop put the wrong parts on your car? What does that mean? What parts?" The customer says, "Ahh, the fender I think." "Well, what's wrong with that part?" and he says, "Well look, I have a Ford. And they say you told them to put some part on that wasn't a Ford. It was manufactured by some other company. Why would you want to put the wrong parts on my car?" Now for those of you in the auto insurance business, you know what he is probably talking about is after-market parts. This is a perfectly reasonable repair. But is there a chance, just a chance, that when the customer called the body shop and said, "Hey, is my car ready?" they said, "Yeah, it's ready. By the way, your insurance company said to put on an after-market part." And the customer said, "After-market, what's that?" "Oh, that just means a part not manufactured by Ford." And now the customer says, "What! They're going to put the wrong parts on my car!" And guess what, by the time he's calling the adjuster back, he's not using the word *after-market* anymore. Guess what word he's using? That's right, *wrong*.

Ask why

The first step in dealing with angry people is to ask *why*. What went wrong? You need get that out. Believe it or not, the first step is not to apologize because you can't apologize for something you don't know went wrong. So, ask them, "Why are you angry? What went wrong?" And of course, the customer will tell you. Once the customer says it, like in this case, "You told the body shop to put the wrong parts on my car," now is the time to apologize. But think about it. Wait a minute. Why are we apologizing? We didn't do anything wrong. Did you think we did this? Did you think we called up the shop and said, "Hey, by the way, put the wrong parts on this guy's car." That ought to be a hoot. We probably didn't do this, so why are we apologizing? Because the customer *thinks* we did. So right now, we want to calm this guy down.

Apologize

So, the solution is to say, "You know what, if we put the wrong parts on your car, I certainly apologize. We didn't want to do that." You're letting the customer know that even if it happened, it was a mistake. You see, part of the reason this customer is angry is he thinks whatever you did wrong, you did it on purpose. So, let him know it was a mistake. If it happened, we're sorry, that's not what we want.

Refocus

The third step and the powerful one we were telling you about before is called *refocus*. Refocus the customer to let them know, even if it did happen, it was an accident, and normally things go better. An appropriate response might be something along the lines of, "You know what, if we told the body shop to put the wrong parts on your car, that was a mistake and we certainly don't want to do that. Our goal is to make sure your car gets fixed properly. That's our goal." See, to refocus someone is to remind them that normally, we're pretty good. If you don't do this, it's almost admitting that it happens all the time. Think about this. Let's say someone were to call you up and they say, "You know what, you people never return your phone calls," and your response is, "Yeah, what's your point?" Isn't that kind of admitting it happens all the time? Well, if we don't refocus customers to let them know, even if it happened it was an accident, because we want to do the right thing, we're almost admitting yes, we screw things up all the time. And we don't want to do that. So, it's a very important step to refocus the customer to let them know we're trying to do the right thing.

Gather the facts

So far, we have three steps: ask why, apologize and refocus. Step number four is *gather the facts*. Notice in this scenario we gave you, had the adjuster taken the time to gather the facts, they wouldn't have made any phone calls. They would have just explained to the customer what was going on. But we tend not to do that. Why? Because when customers are angry, we're in such a hurry to get off the phone and solve the problem, oftentimes we don't even know what the problem is. Here's a good hint and one that we like to share with our adjusters. If you can't even tell what the problem is or it doesn't even make sense, like in this case, hang on. Don't hang up the phone. Keep talking. Find out what's really wrong and get all of the facts. Now the problem with doing this is, when people are angry, do they want to be questioned? Do they want to give a lot of information? No. They don't want to. That's why you have to calm them down by apologizing and refocusing them, letting them know we're trying to help them and maybe they will be a little freer with the information.

Initiate a plan of action

The final step is to *initiate a plan of action*. Let the customer know what you are going to do to help them. A plan of action could be as simple as "Let me now take the time to explain to you why we did this." A plan of action could be "Let me call the body shop and I'll call you back by four o'clock." A plan of action could be "Let me check with my supervisor, we'll check case law, we'll send you a letter, you should have it within two weeks." Some plan of action that the customer can now know this is what's going to happen and set an expectation very clearly. In this case, in this scenario that we just described, we think the adjuster could have handled the entire situation in one conversation. Imagine this.

Let's say the adjuster had his five steps down. The customer calls up and screams, "You guys are a bunch of idiots! What's wrong with you!" and the adjuster says, "Sir, can you tell me what happened?" "Yeah, you told the body shop to put the wrong parts on my car." "You know what, sir, if we did that (told the body shop to put the wrong parts on your car) I'm certainly sorry. We want the right parts on your car. I mean, that's our goal, to make sure thinks get done right. I'm sorry it didn't happen." "Yeah, fine whatever." "Let me ask you a couple of questions, sir. In order to help you, let me understand this problem. What part was it?" "Oh, it was the fender." "Can you tell me what was wrong with it?" "Well, I've got a Ford and they told me that you told them to put on some part made by somebody else." "Ahh... well, that means an after-market part was used, sir." "Yeah, that's the word they used." "OK, let me go ahead and explain what that means, why it's an acceptable repair, and why we use after-market parts. Do you have a moment so I can explain that to you?" And guess what, that adjuster could have avoided all of those phone calls. Who knows? But those five steps are very powerful in calming down an angry customer and saving you some time and improving customer service. Just because a customer is angry, doesn't mean they are a bad customer. They're still good customers, and we've got a great chance of improving retention and holding on to them by exceeding their expectations because they think they are going to get a bunch of excuses.

The five steps in dealing with angry customers are:

1. Ask why. Ask why, so you know what's going on.

2. Apologize. In a general sense, apologize. We didn't want this to go wrong.

3. Refocus. Let the customer know that if it happened, we certainly didn't mean for it to happen. We want things to go right.

4. Gather the facts. Make sure you've got all the information you need to help the customer.

5. Initiate a plan of action. Tell the customer what you are going to do to help them.

AWESOME CLAIMS CUSTOMER SERVICE

Now we have a new scenario coming up. It's a role play. And what we want to do is have you look at this and see how the adjuster does in this case.

Adjuster (Dave): "Hi, this is Dave with International Insurance, can I help you?"

Customer (Jane Ryan): "Dave, this is Jane Ryan, we spoke earlier, and I am really irritated today."

Adjuster: "Ahh, can I ask you what your problem is?"

Customer: "What is *my* problem? My problem is that your car company that you recommended was supposed to have a car here by four o'clock today and it is four thirty. I took off work and now I am still stuck. What are you going to do about it?"

Adjuster: "Wow, that seems like quite an issue. You know, I'm not really sure."

Customer: "What do you mean, 'you're not really sure?'"

Adjuster: "Well, I mean it's not really something I have control over."

Customer: "Don't you have a relationship with these people. Don't you do business with them?"

Adjuster: "Well sure, all the time, yeah..."

Customer: "Well then, why don't you get them to bring a car to me now? I'm here now!"

Adjuster: "Well, I'll tell you what, why don't I go ahead and give them a call and I'll call you right back."

Customer: "Yeah, you better."

How did the adjuster do? Well, not too good. You know, we have got to ask why, but do it politely. You have to ask politely, "Can you tell me why you're upset? Can you tell me what happened?" Nice and polite. Notice what happened in this case, "What's your problem" didn't go over too well, did it?

What we have to do is find out why. Do it in a polite manner. In this case, since the adjuster didn't do a good job of apologizing or calming the customer down, he now has to call the rental agency without a lot of information. What information would you think he should have asked for? Who was supposed to drop off the car? Where? What time? Lots of information he could have gathered, but he didn't. Why? Because he didn't do a good job of apologizing and refocusing the customer in order to calm the customer down long enough so he could get the information he needs to solve the problem.

AWESOME CLAIMS CUSTOMER SERVICE

You can just imagine what happened in this conversation, can't you. The adjuster calls up the rental agency, talks to Alicia, the Branch Manager and says, "Hey Alicia, I've got a customer, says you were supposed to drop off a car, here's the customer's name." Alicia says, "Oh, well her husband called up and wanted the car dropped off at his work so we did that." "Oh, you did." "Oh yeah, we already did." "Ok, well, thanks." Now you call the customer back and tell her the car has already been dropped off. Do you think she's going to be happy? No, she's going to be mad. She's going to be mad that she wasn't contacted. And you know what, we actually did something in that process of trying to help the customer that is really bad customer service.

We are in the customer service business. That means that we have to make sure everybody does their part as far as customer service. When we were talking to Alicia, guess what we should have told Alicia? "You know what Alicia, if her husband called up and said he wanted the car dropped off and you did, that's fine. But you should have called my customer. You should have called her and told her that," and Alicia says, "Well, we can't help it if husbands and wives don't talk to each other." Our response would be, "Well, you know what Alicia, that doesn't matter. What *does* matter is the customer was at home waiting for the car and didn't know you dropped it off. You should have called her and told her that. Because you didn't, I got this phone call. I already work until 5:30, and I don't want to work until 6:00." We wouldn't be mean to her but would let her know that because she didn't do this, she caused extra work for you. In claims, sometimes we let our vendors get away with delivering bad customer service, and we pay the price. We have to make sure that doesn't happen by insisting on outstanding customer service from our vendors at all times.

You might be thinking, "Why should we apologize to the customer? We didn't do anything wrong." Well think about it. If we didn't do anything wrong, then why is the customer mad at us? Well, who probably referred this rental agency to the customer? We probably did, right? So, if the vendor doesn't do something they are supposed to do, it's perfectly reasonable for the customer to be angry at us. What we have to do is respond by accepting responsibility and being involved in solving the problem. We have another role play here. We hope the adjuster does better this time. You tell us.

Adjuster (Dave): "Hello, this is Dave with International Insurance. Can I help you?"

Customer (Jane Ryan): "Dave, this is Jane Ryan. We spoke earlier today, and I am so angry. I am having a real problem."

AWESOME CLAIMS CUSTOMER SERVICE

Adjuster: "Mrs. Ryan, I am sorry to hear that. Can you tell me why you're angry?"

Customer: "Yeah, I can tell you why I'm angry. That car company that you recommended has not shown up with my car and they promised it to me by four o'clock today and here it is, it's four thirty."

Adjuster: "Mrs. Ryan, I apologize if they said they would be there by four o'clock and they weren't. I know that can be quite frustrating. This car company we recommend to our customers is actually quite good at what they do and if they didn't deliver in this case, I apologize for that. Can you tell me specifically what time range they might have given you to deliver the car?"

Customer: "Well, all I know is, they said it was going to be by four o'clock."

Adjuster: "Oh, OK, do you remember, perhaps, who you spoke to?"

Customer: "I do, I spoke to a woman named Alicia."

Adjuster: "OK, yes, I know Alicia at the local branch. Why don't I do this for you, Mrs. Ryan, I'll give Alicia a call, figure out what's going on, it's four thirty now, if I can call you back by five o'clock this afternoon, would that be OK?"

Customer: "That would be fine."

Adjuster: "OK, let me go ahead and take care of this for you and I'll call you back by five."

Customer: "Thank you Dave. I appreciate anything you could do to help."

One thing in there we really like is where Dave says, "Normally, they do a pretty good job, that's why we use them." Well think about it. That's a refocus statement, isn't it? He's letting them know we use this company because normally they are pretty good. See, a good reason for the customer to be angry is that we just refer them to this company because we don't care about customer service. We just use them because they are cheap. And what did he do? He refocused the customer to let the customer know we use them because normally, they do a very good job. That's enough to calm a customer down and get enough information so you can help them.

So, remember the five tips on dealing with angry people:

1. Ask why. Find out what happened.

2. Apologize. Apologize in a general way or in a broad sense.

3. Refocus. Let the customer know that it usually doesn't go wrong and that your company usually does a good job.

4. Gather the facts. Make sure the customer believes and understands you're trying to help.

5. Initiate an action plan. Propose a plan of action that will solve the problem.

The Follow-Up Call

The *nothing went right* customer:

Sometimes you have a situation in which, despite everyone's best effort, nothing goes right. Once the problems have been corrected, the customer should be called to determine if everything is satisfactory. The customer will usually appreciate this courtesy and perhaps remember.

The *irate* customer:

When you hang up from a conversation with an irate customer, the last thing you want to do is speak with that customer again. Whether the cause of the complaint was legitimate or questionable, a follow-up call is a good idea. By calling to ask if the action you initiated was satisfactory, you will pleasantly surprise the customer and perhaps it will be remembered.

This *new* customer:

When you provide service to a new customer, it's a good time to extend an extra courtesy. Make a follow-up call to learn if everything is satisfactory. The customer's perception of your company will be enhanced and perhaps, they will remember. Remember what? Remember when it's time to renew their policy, they received outstanding customer service.

A Few Telephone Tips

The standard greeting: There are four parts of a standard telephone greeting and these apply especially in claims.

1. Greet the caller

2. State your organization or your department

3. Introduce yourself

4. Offer your help

AWESOME CLAIMS CUSTOMER SERVICE

Instead of just saying, "Claims," you might want to say, "Good morning this is _____ Insurance. This is Carl Van; may I help you?"

Develop a strategy for closing a customer interaction. The five common parts for a standard telephone closing are:

1. Thank the customer for calling or meeting with you.

2. Let the customer know you want him or her to feel comfortable.

3. Provide any assurance that makes sense that the promises will be fulfilled.

4. Set expectations around the process using the values and the benefits to the customer.

5. Leave the customer with a positive feeling.

A good example would be, "Thank you for your time, Mr. Smith. As I mentioned, our goal at _____ Insurance is to make sure that you understand the process. I hope you feel comfortable now," or "Those were good questions, Mr. Smith. Thank you. I hope the answers have helped you understand the process."

CHAPTER 13

The Opportunity to Help People

Well it's time to talk about *attitude*. Don't roll your eyes. Don't worry. We're not going to get on our attitude soap boxes. We know people worry about that. We're not going to talk about attitude like being happy all the time. We're going to be talking about attitude and how it relates to providing outstanding customer service. Many performance management experts talk about attitude being a very important element in overall job performance. They are not defining attitude as being happy. They are talking about whether someone has the right attitude toward their job. Do they understand how important and sophisticated their job is? Do they understand the real responsibilities which come with their job? This is the attitude they are talking about. And we are going to relate that in claims to make our job a little bit easier and improve customer service.

Alright, what we'd like you to do now is take a little attitude quiz. Take a moment and think about each of the following statements. Are they true or false?

1. **Your attitude towards your customers influences your behavior. You cannot always camouflage how you feel.**

What did you come up with? We happen to think this statement is true. Carl was giving a speech once on customer service and had a claims representative come up to him after the speech to tell him he disagreed with what he had said.

"Well, what part exactly?" Carl asked.

"Well, the part about treating people with respect."

"You disagree with that?"

"Yes, and that you have to be extra patient with people."

"You disagree with that, that you have to be extra patient with people?"

"Yes, I disagree."

"Well, why would you disagree with that?"

"Because you're talking about the enemy."

Think about this — If his attitude is the customer is the enemy, is there just a chance he's treating them that way? Is it just possible his attitude comes out in his words, in his communication and how he treats the customer? We think so. Most of us aren't that bad. If we adopt the attitude that we are in the business of providing customer service —this is what we do—then we will instinctively treat our customers differently.

2. **"Your attitude determines your level of job satisfaction."**

What's your answer? Ours is, true. We *do* believe a person's attitude determines their level of job satisfaction. We have had tremendous claims people working for us over the years and those that did a fantastic job knew their job was customer service. That was their attitude and they always had a high level of job satisfaction. Not everybody who has worked for us has had this insight. For example, Mike was a good technician. One day he came up to Carl and said, "Carl, this just isn't a job for me."

"Well, what do you want Mike? What kind of job are you looking for?"

"I want a job where I have responsibility."

"Responsibility? You're practically holding people's lives in your hands. What are you talking about?"

"Well, I want a job where I have authority."

"Authority? You can write a check for twenty thousand dollars without blinking. How many of your college buddies can do that with their company's money?"

"Well, I want a job where I can help people."

"Help people? Mike, your job is to help people. This is what you do. These people do need help."

"No, they just whine and cry and complain."

"Well Mike, what do people do when they need help? What does a job like that look like?"

Sometimes we have to recognize the opportunity we have. Not everybody can do this job. We've had good claims people say, "Oh, this is a tough job. You've got to deal with doctors and lawyers and technical people and body shops, and vendors and you've got to deal with all these different people. This is a tough job." And we say, "You're right. This is a very tough job. That's why we hired you. That's why you have this job and not somebody else. If this were an easy job, we wouldn't need talented people. We need you." Keep this in mind because claims is a tough business but then again, there's opportunity in that as well.

3. **Your attitude affects everyone who comes in contact with you, either in person, or on the telephone.**

What do you think? We put down true for this one. Did you? We are firm believers that our attitude does affect everyone we encounter. Here's an example.

Carl was just sitting on a plane minding his own business when this guy walks in. He has his ticket in his hand, and he walks up to the flight attendant who is standing in front of Carl. This is at the very front of the plane. He sticks the ticket in the flight attendant's face and says, "Where should I sit?"

AWESOME CLAIMS CUSTOMER SERVICE

"Well sir, I don't know where you should sit. How would I know where you're sitting?"

"Well, don't you know where everybody sits? Are you that bad of an airline? Are you that unorganized? You don't even know where people are sitting?"

"Sir, we can't know where every single person is sitting. What does your ticket say?"

"It says 11 E,"

"Well, it's probably right down there past 10 E."

"Fine."

The guy stomps away. So, this guy is a jerk right? You might be thinking that — Carl kind of was too. Meanwhile, the flight attendant, who wasn't doing anything wrong, is upset because somebody threw an attitude at her. So, guess what she does next? She gets on the microphone, clicks it on, and starts yelling at this guy but everyone is getting yelled at.

"Everyone must be seated. We cannot pull away from the gate unless every single person is seated."

Of course, he's the only one standing. Then she hangs up the microphone and looks at Carl and says, "What a jerk." Then she turns to her co-worker and says, "See that guy down in 11 E, that guy is a jerk. Don't give him any orange juice." So now they're going to play the old orange juice deprivation trick.

Her reaction was perfectly reasonable based upon what she knew. She wasn't doing anything wrong and this guy comes in and blasts her. So, she fights back. Why should she have to take his abuse?

However, if she'd been in the terminal 30, maybe 45 minutes, before we got on the plane, like Carl was, her reaction would most likely have been different. This guy actually had his wife and child with him—a two, maybe three-year-old girl. He goes up to the ticket counter while they go to the gate. Because the airline is understaffed, he's waiting at the ticket counter until someone finally gets there and tells him he is supposed to be at the gate. So, he goes running up to the gate.

"I've got to get on the plane. My wife and daughter are on the plane, I've got to get on the plane."

"Well sir, we gave away your seat."

"You gave away my seat! How could you do that?"

AWESOME CLAIMS CUSTOMER SERVICE

"Well sir, you've got to be here fifteen minutes before the flight takes off."

"How am I supposed to know that?"

"Well sir, didn't you read your flight ticket?" (Who does that, right? But don't we always tell this to customers? "Didn't you read your policy?")

"No, I didn't read it, but I've got to get on the plane."

"Well sir, we gave away your seat. There is nothing we can do."

"Look, I've got to get on this plane."

"Well sir, you can go ahead and fly tomorrow. We've got one seat on the flight tomorrow." (It's Friday, and Monday is a holiday, so it's booked solid.)

"I can't do that. I've got reservations. I've got the credit card. My wife doesn't even know where we are staying,"

"Well sir, we can pull your wife and daughter off, and you can fly on Sunday."

"I can't do that. The cruise is going to leave and that would ruin our whole vacation."

He gets madder and madder and she keeps saying, "Sir, this isn't our fault." Now every time she says, "Sir, this isn't our fault," guess what she is really saying? "This is *your* fault," and he gets madder and madder and finally she decides she's done talking with him. She pulls a coworker over and says, "Hey Julie, can you talk to this guy?" Julie walks over, and the whole process starts over again. "This isn't our fault. This isn't our fault." All the excuses, everything going on, and this poor guy is getting madder and madder and madder.

At some point, it dawns on him; he's not getting on the plane, it's not going to happen. And you know what? Just the thought that his wife and little girl were going to be in some strange city alone, without him, was breaking this guy down to his core. Carl thought he was going to break down right there at the counter. He was holding on to the counter and shaking, and they kept saying, "This isn't our fault. This isn't our fault."

Right about this time, Carl got on the plane. He felt terrible for this man. Maybe he would have given him his seat if he didn't need to get home. So, Carl's sitting there in his seat, near the front of the plane, feeling bad for this person and guess who boards the plane? Somehow, miracle of miracles, this poor guy got a seat. He comes walking in and guess who gets in his way? Some poor flight attendant who's never met him. He blasts her and she fights back. Now the guy is not going to get his orange juice. Was she wrong for the way she reacted? The way she reacted was perfectly reasonable. She got yelled at and she didn't deserve it but that's what happens sometimes. Is this guy a jerk? Hard to say. He was acting like a jerk but that's what people do when they get upset. That's what happens when people get thrown into a situation they didn't want, don't like, and didn't ask for. He took it out on her, and he shouldn't have. Nevertheless, if she had seen what Carl saw and had any compassion, her reaction would have been quite different.

"You know what sir, I'm so sorry what you just went through. I saw it and I apologize for the fact that you had that difficulty. Let me show you to your seat. Let me see if I can get your wife and daughter near you. Let me buy you a drink."

We are not sure exactly what she would say, but we know her response would have been different. She would have had a level of empathy that she didn't have because she didn't see what happened before.

Why is this important for us in claims? Because this is how we get our customers. We get our customers after something bad has happened to them, something they didn't want, don't like, and didn't ask for; after they had rules enforced upon them that they had nothing to do with. No, it's not fair that sometimes they take it out on us. But these are the people we said we would help.

4. Your attitude is reflected not only by your tone of voice, but also by the way you sit, stand, facial expressions, and other non-verbal ways.

Our answer to this statement tends to lean toward true. You know, when we are talking to a customer service person on the phone, we can almost tell when they have their hand on their head and they are typing one finger at a time. Our customers deserve our full attention, not to be distracted by co-workers trying to talk to us while we're talking to our customers.

5. Your attitude is not fixed. The attitude you choose to display is up to you.

This statement can be debated. We've heard arguments over this. Some people say no, you have no control over your attitude. Your attitude is basically molded by the things that happen to you. Other people say yes, you can change your attitude and if you do, your job satisfaction will increase. Well, let's talk about this further.

We want to tell you about a claims person that used to work for Carl. Her name was Rochelle. She starts off the book *The 8 Characteristics of the Awesome Adjuster*. One day, she was sitting in the break room reading her claims law book, minding her own business. As Carl came walking in, he heard a coworker say something to her. "You know what, it's just not fair that Carl makes you do all this extra work. He's always giving you all these extra assignments, giving you all this extra work. You should say something to him. He should spread that around." Now keep in mind, Carl heard this. And right then, Rochelle, who was reading her book, looks up at this person and says, "You know what, I know Carl gives me a lot of extra work to do. He gives me a lot of extra responsibilities. He must trust me and think highly of me to do that. And when people think highly of me, I work hard not to let them down." Then she went back to reading her claims law book.

Now of course, Carl resisted the urge to drop to his knees and bow down saying, "I'm not worthy, I'm not worthy." You know what, that was a pretty good response. Somehow, Rochelle had the ability to recognize opportunity when she saw it. Instead of seeing a bunch of hard work, she saw the opportunity. "Here was an opportunity to show someone who had faith in me that their faith isn't misplaced." We can tell you; Carl didn't give her this attitude. She seemed to have it. And because of that, she had a high level of job satisfaction. Now her response was about a million times better than Carl's response because three weeks earlier, something happened to him that was quite different.

Carl was in his boss's office and was complaining and whining saying things like, "Hey, I'm working all these extra hours, I've got all this extra responsibility. The other branch managers aren't doing this, HR gave me this project and I had to spend all last Saturday..." Carl's whining and complaining, figuring he's bound to get a company car out of this or something, right? His boss is just staring at him, waiting for Carl to wear himself out and finish so he can speak.

"Carl, are you done?"

"Yeah, I'm done."

"Good, because I want to remind you of something Carl."

"What?"

"You asked for this job, remember? Carl, you sat here in this office, you practically begged me for this job. Twenty-three people applied for this job, Carl, and you got it. You're the one who told me you were the only one I could possibly hire. Tell you what, you want an easy job? Go to McDonald's. A little buzzer goes off when the fries have to come up, OK? If that's what you want, go ahead, do it. But before you leave my office, Carl, I want to remind you, not only did you ask for this job, but you got something twenty-two other people didn't get. You got the chance to prove that you could do this job, because no one else even got the chance."

His speech wasn't "Let's Go Win One for the Gipper;" it was "Get Out of My Office Because You Begged Me for This Job." You know what, he was right. Somehow, Carl's boss recognized the extra work and challenges he was given were the very things he had wanted. Carl wanted the responsibility. He wanted the respect and the authority. He wanted the money. He wanted the title. However, once he got those things, his thoughts were oh my goodness, look at all this hard work. Rochelle recognized the extra work and challenges Carl was giving her were his outward expression that he believed in her more than anybody else. Carl was the only one in the mix not getting it.

How was Rochelle able to identify opportunity? Well, you know, there's an old saying which goes something like this: "The trouble with opportunity is it's disguised as hard work." And there's no place where that's truer than in the claims world. We live in a tough environment. We have a tough job. But again, that's where the opportunity comes from because most people couldn't do the job we do. To focus on that can be very helpful and make our jobs easier. In order to give you a little clue about how to do that, we want to tell you a short story called *Acres of Diamonds*.

In his book, *The Psychology of Achievement*, Brian Tracy does a great job of paraphrasing *Acres of Diamonds* and presenting a moral. It's about an old African farmer at the turn of the century and he's doing pretty well on his farm. One day he hears about people discovering diamond mines and becoming fabulously wealthy. So, he sells his land and tools and all of his animals, and he heads off in search of diamond mines.

Well 12, 13, 15 years later, broke, destitute, and alone, he throws himself into the ocean and drowns. Meanwhile, back on the old farm, a new farmer, who's watering down his donkey in a stream, looks down and he sees a rock—a rock that reflects light in a remarkable way. So, he picks up the rock, takes it into town, and shows it to someone who knows what it is.

"Well, this is a diamond."

"It's a diamond! It doesn't look like a diamond."

"Well, no, you've got to press it, and shape it, and cut it, but it's a diamond. Can you take me back to where you found it?"

"Sure."

So, they head back to the farm and the farmer looks down and he sees another rock. He picks that up and that's a diamond. He sees another rock, he picks that up and that's a diamond. Lo and behold, he looks up and he realizes he's literally standing on acres of diamonds. Now the moral of that story isn't look under your own two feet. The moral of that story is if you're going to look for something, you better know what it's going to look like when you find it.

Remember Carl's adjuster Mike? Somehow, he had gotten lost in all the hard work, and he didn't recognize the job that he wanted—opportunity, authority, responsibility, the ability to help people—was the job he already had.

Here's a suggestion from us on this issue: Every once in a while, not every day, but every once in a while, stay focused on the fact that you have an opportunity to help people. That's a great opportunity, one that many people don't have in their careers. We have an opportunity to help people, where something bad has happened to them. They didn't want it, they don't like it, and they didn't ask for it, but we get to help them. Remember, we have a tough job. But also, we have the opportunity to be involved in helping people. Stay focused on that and you know what, your level of job satisfaction will go up and your focus on your customers will increase.

Attitude and Ability

So, how much of your performance is actually tied into attitude? Well, many performance management experts will say that you can break down people's performance into two categories: attitude and ability. What percentages would you think they would assign to these two things? Think about it for a second.

Most performance management experts will tell you that performance is made up of approximately 80 percent attitude and 20 percent ability. Most people come up with figures close to that. Now again, we're not talking about attitude meaning one is happy all the time. We're talking about your attitude toward your job. In the case of claims, do you understand that you're in a customer service business? If your attitude is "this is the job that I do," you will excel at that particular job. Here's what we mean.

Carl was teaching a customer service class for claims people and everybody was kind of getting involved, but there was one student who was really focusing and going out of his way to practice extra hard. He was writing and taking notes like crazy, and Carl said to him, "Wow, you really seem to be taking to this," and he said, "Well, sure, this is my life's work." Based upon his attitude, you would have thought he was developing a cure for cancer. Carl was very impressed. That is not something Carl would normally say. The student saw it this way: I'm a claims adjuster and my job is to help people. Because this is my life's work, I might as well be outstanding at it.

Let's think about this further. If his attitude is dealing with customers and helping them is his life's work, is there a chance he deals with people differently than the person who sees his customers as the enemy? Well, it's possible we are all guilty of sometimes feeling like the customer is the enemy. We agree with that. We're all human beings. In this case, this person's attitude was that helping people is his life's work. And you know what, he had a much easier time with his customers, and he excelled not because of his ability but because of his attitude.

CHAPTER 14

Changing Carl's Attitude

We would like to tell you about the time Carl's job as a claims adjuster became so much easier. A lot of people believe it's perfectly harmless to say things like this customer is a "jerk," this guy is an "idiot," and these people are "morons." This is all perfectly fine as long as you hang up first and the customer doesn't hear you. Carl would have to plead guilty—this is one of the things he used to do when he was a claims adjuster. As a matter of fact, one of his favorite things to do was to run around the office and tell everybody about the jerk he had just spoken with. Can this be damaging? Well, it might be, and we want to tell you why. Like the title of this chapter said, we want to tell you about the day Carl's job as a claims adjuster became so much easier.

AWESOME CLAIMS CUSTOMER SERVICE

Carl was a total loss adjuster and had a supervisor by the name of Steve. Steve was Carl's target for all of this running around calling customers names. He would run over to Steve and say, "Hey Steve, you wouldn't believe what this idiot just said," and he was in on it. He would say, "What, what did he say, Carl?" and he'd tell him, and they'd laugh. It was a great bonding experience, really. And this went on for three years. He was Carl's supervisor for three years and he used to do this all the time. No harm because the customer never heard Carl say anything behind their backs, right? And guess what? One day, Carl got a new supervisor. This guy's name was Doug. And Carl couldn't make Doug laugh for the life of him. No matter what Carl would say to him, he never thought anything was funny. And then all of a sudden, something amazing happened. One day, Carl was settling a total loss on a brand-new Corvette.

So, this is a brand-new Corvette, just driven off the lot, and the poor guy got into an accident. Of course, Carl had to explain about the fact that it depreciated as soon as he drove it off the lot and all that kind of stuff. It took Carl a while to settle this case. It took him a good forty-five minutes, maybe an hour, going back and forth, back and forth. And then finally, Carl settled it. And he hung up, thinking, "Boy that took a while." And guess what? He called Carl back fifteen minutes later.

"Mr. Van, I've got a question for you."

"What. What could you possibly want to know?"

"Well, you said you were going to pay me for the value of the car, right?"

"Yeah, I did."

"Well, I had just filled up the tank with gas before this accident happened. Are you going to pay me for the gas too?"

Carl thought, "Oh my goodness, what a moron."

So, Carl goes running over to Doug. He's thinking this story is going to make him laugh.

"Hey Doug, you won't believe what this idiot just said,"

"OK, Carl, fine. You caught somebody saying something stupid in a claim. Congratulations, Carl, big wow. Now that you've accomplished this feat, what are you going to do to help this guy?"

"Help him? Help him do what?"

"Why don't you help him understand he got what he's entitled to? Why don't you help him understand we treated him fairly? Why don't you help him understand he doesn't have to feel violated a second time? If this guy feels so out of control that a tank of gas is going to make him feel whole, maybe he doesn't need you making fun of him behind his back. Maybe, he just needs some help."

Crash, here comes the ton of bricks. Think about it. In one conversation, Carl's new supervisor let him know, "Carl, you're not here to make fun of customers. We're not paying you to do that. Your job is to help people." And to be honest, Carl was a claims adjuster for three years before anybody ever referred to his job as helping people. This was nowhere in his job objectives, and it didn't show up in his performance reviews. And you know what? His conversation with Doug had a profound impact on him. You know why? He likes helping people. He likes it. He's not a nut. He doesn't drive up and down the road looking for people with flats. But if somebody came up to him and said, "Hey, my battery is dead, would you give me jump?" "Sure." He likes helping people. It's a lot more fun than beating them up.

From that day forward, Carl's job became so much easier. Why? Because now he realized his job was to help people. He would start using those words. Now when they were yelling at him, it didn't seem so bad because, guess what? He's here to help them. Instead of saying, "You have to move your car or we are going to charge you for the fees," Carl would now say, "Let me help you understand why moving your vehicle will help you." Instead of saying, "If you don't send in that medical form, you're not getting paid," he would now say, "I appreciate you don't want to do that. Let me show you how this can help you." He would just start using the word "help" quite a bit. When he did that, Carl found his customers trusted him and were much more cooperative. It was the biggest change in his career.

So, is it so bad that we run around calling customers names? Does it really hurt? Well, we'll tell you this: There is no great customer service company that allows this. It doesn't exist. As a matter of fact, even the idea that we can deliver outstanding customer service while the customer service people themselves are free to run around and call customers names behind their backs, is so ludicrous, you can't even describe it in words. It's simply not possible. How we talk to our customers and how we talk to each other about our customers influences our behavior because it changes our attitude. And what is eighty percent of our performance? Attitude.

CHAPTER 15

Telephone Techniques to Avoid

This next section is something we like to call *telephone techniques to avoid*. When Carl monitors phone calls, he hears good adjusters sometimes innocently saying something that could really come off as bad customer service. So, he likes to write them down and we have a few for you today. What we want to do is go over a couple of them and then have you change some of them as we go through them. On this first one, Carl was monitoring a phone call and heard somebody ask for Mr. Lark. The person who was talking to the customer said, "I am sorry, Mr. Lark is still at lunch." Well, what's the problem with that?

AWESOME CLAIMS CUSTOMER SERVICE

Well, obviously, it's the word *still*. What does that mean, *still* at lunch? Well, Carl went out and found out. You know what, Mr. Lark was only gone for 15 minutes. But when somebody said he's *still* at lunch, what does that sound like? How long does this guy get? What should we say instead? We'd probably just say, "Mr. Lark is at lunch. He'll be back by one o'clock," something innocent like that.

The next one was this: Somebody had called up and asked for someone named Tom and was told, "We don't know where Tom is." We don't know where he is. What's the problem with that? Sounds a little unorganized, right? Sounds like we don't know where our employees are. We don't know where Tom is. We saw him digging up turnips in the garden last week. That's all we know. What you could say instead is, "Tom's away from his desk. Can I help you?" Something along those lines.

Another one Carl likes which he heard was, "Oh, Debra is in the middle of a big customer problem right now. Can I have her call you?" What's the problem with that? Well, there are a couple problems with this one. The first one, the most glaring, Debra is in the middle of a big customer problem. Here's a hint. If you have big customer problems, don't broadcast it to the rest of your customers. That's number one. But number two, it could easily make this person feel like their problem isn't important, right? So, what should we say instead?

"Debra's helping another customer right now. Can I have her call you, or can I help you?" Sound better?

Alright, we are going to give you a statement and this time, what we want you to do is identify what is wrong. What bad customer service impression could it leave? And more importantly, what would you say instead? We really want you to focus on what's wrong with this statement and what could be said instead.

Carl heard somebody say, "Oh, Jack is fishing somewhere." The customer wanted to talk to Jack and was told Jack is fishing somewhere. Now we know this person is saying Jack's on vacation but what we want you to do is write down what bad impression could it leave and what you would say instead. Give it a try.

What's the problem with this one? Besides being a little unprofessional, should we be telling customers what we're doing? Carl hears this quite frequently. He hears good adjusters say, "Oh, Sally's off getting her molars pulled" or "Susie's picking her kids up from day care." Do we really need to tell our customers what we are doing and where we are? Probably not—our suggestion would be, "Jack is on vacation. Can I help you?"

On this next one, a customer called up and wanted to talk to an adjuster. And guess what? She was told, "Oh, she went home early." Think about it for a second. What's wrong with it and how would you say it instead. Go ahead.

Our guess is you came up with something like, well, it kind of sounds like maybe she's a slacker or she ran out of work. Not a good impression. She went home early. She had nothing else to do. What would be a better approach? Our suggestion would be, "She's gone for the day. Can I help you or can I have her call you?" Nice and simple.

Next one. "Oh, that department takes forever to answer the phone." Somebody actually said this to a customer. "That department takes forever to answer the phone." What's wrong with it? What would you say instead? Go ahead.

What's wrong with that? Maybe they do take a long time to answer the phone. The problem is, can you ever gain credibility by cutting down another department in your company? You really can't. It will always look bad. Here's our suggestion: just say something along the lines of, "I apologize you've had difficulty with that department. Let me see if I could help you."

The next one. Somebody told a customer, "Sir, you are going to have to understand." What's wrong with that and what would you say instead?

What's wrong with that? To tell someone they are going to have to do something, what did we say before? That plants a seed in their mind that they won't like it. By the way, when you say something like, "You are going to have to understand," aren't you kind of calling them stupid? "You're going to have to understand," as if they're too dumb. What would be a better way to say that? "Sir, I hope you'll understand." "It's important for you to understand." "I'd like for you to understand." That's a whole lot better than "You are going to have to understand."

"Well, sir, that's not how I deal with it." What's the problem with that? Go ahead.

Is there a problem with "That's not how I deal with it?" Yes. What you don't want to do is imply that you set company policy. If you say something like this to a customer, "That's not how I deal with it," then he thinks he's just got the bad luck of having you. Maybe if he got somebody else, he'd get a better response. You're probably better off saying something like, "That's not how it's done" or "This is company policy," something that makes it sound like you're not the one making the bad decision against that person.

How about this one: A customer was told, "You know, it sounds like you're confused." Tell me what's wrong with it and what you would say instead.

AWESOME CLAIMS CUSTOMER SERVICE

There's little doubt here. We're calling the customer stupid. "You're confused." The problem also is that we're not accepting responsibility. It's not the customer's job to understand us. It's our job to make sure we clearly explain to a customer. One of the hallmarks of great customer service people is that they accept responsibility. "It's my job to make sure this is clear." Had that adjuster had that level of responsibility, he wouldn't have said, "It sounds like you're confused." He would have said, "Maybe I haven't explained this clearly. Let me try again." That's probably the better response. Well, let's go ahead and move into our next section now.

CHAPTER 16

Claims is a Customer Service Business

We talked before about the words *willing to*, which can make people not want to trust us. We said it would make our job easier if people trusted us and we talked a little bit about the fact that when you say, "We're willing to pay...," it kind of sounds like we really don't want to and we wouldn't if we didn't have to. So, instead of saying, "We're willing to pay you five thousand dollars," you're much better off saying something like, "Your claim is worth five thousand dollars." "We've evaluated your case to five thousand." "We can pay you up to five thousand." This is a good phrase to use instead of *willing to*. We've got a few more we'd like to share with you. One is the word *offer*. We use this word all the time in claims and we're not saying you shouldn't. But many experts do recommend, with unrepresented people, not using the word *offer*. The problem is, when you say, "We're going to offer you five thousand dollars," you may have automatically planted in this person's head, "There's more to come." "This isn't what it's worth, this is just our offer." You're probably better off using a phrase like, "We've evaluated your claim at five thousand dollars." "Your claim is worth five thousand dollars." "We want to settle this for five thousand dollars," rather than throw the word *offer* out. That's going to be hard for people who have been using that word forever. But just think about it. Another word we use all the time is *only*. "Well, I can only pay this." "We can only do this for you." Try to stay away from the word *only*. It lets people know we really can't help them, even though we're trying. Instead of saying, "We can only pay you five thousand dollars," you might say, "We can pay you up to five-thousand." Instead of saying, "We can only pay you twenty-five dollars a day for rental," try "We can pay you up to twenty-five dollars a day for rental."

How about *trust us*? We talked a little bit before about the way to gain trust is to use the word *help*. People trust someone who is trying to help them, and they don't trust someone who is trying to hurt them. Sometimes Carl hears claims people say, "Sir, you are going to have to trust us." That's probably the worst thing you can say, because you're telling the person, "You're not going to like this." If you want someone to trust you, believe it or not, you're better off saying, "Sir, we know you don't have to trust us on this but we want you to understand why we're doing this. You're entitled to understand this," not "Just go with us on blind trust." To let someone know that they don't have to trust you, believe it or not, is the best way to get them to at least consider trusting you.

We've talked a lot about trying to get customers to be reasonable. And we mentioned early on, the worst thing you can say is, "You are going to have to be *reasonable*." It calls them unreasonable. What's the best way to get someone to be reasonable? Well, we had a three-step process, and we went through all three steps. If you want someone to be reasonable, the best thing you can do is convince them you already think they are being reasonable. Remember what we talked about? "You are being reasonable. I understand your point of view." Don't argue the reasons. Argue the facts.

Another one, *you're going to have to be patient*. We hear this all the time when we monitor phone calls. "You're going to have to be patient." This tells somebody they're going to have to do something. You're putting the burden on them. This is the price you will pay for our process. If you want somebody to be patient, no matter

AWESOME CLAIMS CUSTOMER SERVICE

how impatient they've been, try thanking them for their patience. When you thank someone for their patience, believe it or not, they become more patient. "I appreciate how patient you've been." Why? Because people tend to work hard to deserve the compliments you give them. Even if somebody has been on your case every minute, thank them for their patience, and they will probably back off.

Stay calm. We hear this all the time—claims people telling customers to stay calm. You want to upset somebody, tell them to stay calm. You want them to be calm, let them know that being upset is perfectly reasonable. "Mr. Smith, I can certainly appreciate your frustration here. I really do understand it. Thank you for your patience." Give them permission to be upset, and they will calm down.

In this book, you've learned that claims is a customer service business. This is what you do. This is all you do. You've learned ways to increase customer service but also make your job easier. You've learned ways to get the customer to listen better, to remember more of what you said, trust you more, be a little bit more patient, be reasonable, and cooperate better. Apply these skills as best you can, and you will find they are meaningful and directly applicable to your job.

PROFESSIONAL SPEAKING SERVICES

Carl Van is a professional national speaker having delivered presentations throughout the U.S., Canada and the U.K.

His presentation style is upbeat, fast paced and always generates audience participation. He has received numerous recognitions throughout the years, including Most Dynamic Speaker at the national ACE conference.

Mr. Van is qualified to speak on virtually any subject regarding employee performance and customer interaction. Just a few of his Guest Speaking titles include:

General

- Awesome Claims Customer Service: You are Good. You Can Get Better
- How to Avoid Losing Customers

AWESOME CLAIMS CUSTOMER SERVICE

- The Claims Customer Service Standards: 5 Things to Never Forget

- Practical Claims Negotiations: Stop Arguing and Start Agreeing

- Real-Life Time Management for Claims

- Stress Management: Give Yourself a Break Before You Die

- Improving your Attitude and Initiative

- Getting People's Cooperation – A Few Easy Steps

- What Customers Hate – And Why We Do It

- If You Can't Say It Simply and Clearly, Then You Don't Know What You're Talking About: Some Business Writing Basics

- Empathy: The Power Tool of Customer Service

- Why Are They Calling Me? Things to do to Reduce Nuisance Calls

- Let Me Do My Job: Simple Steps to get People to be Patient and Let You Do Your Job

- Trust Me: Effective Ways to Gain Credibility

- Saying No: The Right Way (and easy way), or The Wrong Way (the hard way)

- Claims Listening Skills: How to Avoid Missing the Point

- Teamwork for Claims: Ways to Reduce the Work Created by Individualism

Management

- Handling Your Difficult Employees (Without Threats and Violence)

- Teaching and Coaching for Claims Supervisors and Managers

- Initiative: How to Develop it in Your Staff

- Stop Wasting Your Time – Practical Time Management for Managers

- Effective Delegation: Why People Hate It When You Delegate, and How to Change That

AWESOME CLAIMS CUSTOMER SERVICE

- Managing Change

- Interviewing and Hiring Exceptional Claims Performers

- Motivating Your Team

- How to Make Sure Your Employees get the Most out of Training

- Inspiring Employees to Improve Themselves

For a free DVD, please visit www.CarlVan.org or call 504-393-4570.

"Like" Carl Van on www.Facebook.com/CarlVanSpeaker for updates.

Follow Carl Van on www.Twitter.com/CarlVanSpeaker

IN-PERSON TRAINING SERVICES

Carl Van is President & CEO of International Insurance Institute, Inc. that delivers high quality claims training directly to customers at their locations. He is the author of over 75 technical and soft skill courses that have been delivered to over 100,000 employees throughout the U.S, Canada and the U.K.

Just a few titles of his programs include:

Employee Soft-Skill

- Real-Life Time Management for Claims
- The 8 Characteristics of the Awesome Adjuster
- Claims Negotiation Training
- Conflict Resolution
- Awesome Claims Customer Service

AWESOME CLAIMS CUSTOMER SERVICE

- Managing the Telephone

- Attitude & Initiative Training for the Employee

- Empathy & Listening Skills for Claims

- Employee Organization – Managing the Desk

- Prepare for Promotion – Employee Leadership Training

- Teamwork Basics – No Employee is an Island

- Interpersonal Skills – Improving Team Member Relations

- Effective Recorded Statements

- Business Writing Skills for Employees

- Beating Anxiety and Dealing with Anger – Help for the New Employee

Manager Soft-Skill

- Time Management for Claims Supervisors and Managers

- Coaching and Teaching for Claims Supervisors and Managers
- Keys to Effective Presentations
- Teaching Your Employees the 8 Characteristics of Awesome Employees
- Motivating Your Team
- Handling Difficult Employees
- The New Supervisor
- Interviewing and Hiring Exceptional Claims Performers
- Delegation Training for Supervisors and Managers
- Managing Change
- Team Training
- Leadership Skills for Claims Supervisors and Managers
- Preparing Effective Performance Appraisals
- Managing the Highly Technical Employee

AWESOME CLAIMS CUSTOMER SERVICE

For more information and a free catalog of courses, please visit www.InsuranceInstitute.com or call 504-393-4570.

ON-LINE TRAINING SERVICES

Carl Van is President and owner of Claims Education On-Line website that delivers high quality claims training through streaming video that employees can access anywhere in the world.

He is also available to write, direct and present training courses specific to an individual company or industry. He wrote and presented a claims customer service course on DVD for a national company which was rolled out to all 18,000 employees.

He is the designer, author and presenter of four on-line claims video training courses:

- Exceptional Claims Customer Service

- Negotiation Skills for the Claims Professional

- Real-Life Time Management for Claims

- Critical Thinking for Claims

AWESOME CLAIMS CUSTOMER SERVICE

For more information, visit
www.ClaimsEducationOnLine.com.

EDUCATIONAL ARTICLES BY CARL VAN

Carl Van is owner and publisher of Claims Education Magazine and is the author of numerous articles that have appeared in various periodicals.

Just a sample of articles written by Carl Van:

Van, Carl. "Oh, Her? She's New: A Lesson in Attitude and Performance." Claims Education Magazine. Winter 2011

Van, Carl. "A Lesson in Attitude and Performance." Skin Inc. November 2011

Van, Carl. "Saying 'No' the Right Way." Looking Fit. www.LookingFit.com. May 2011

Van, Carl. "3 Maxims for Successful Negotiation." HVACR Business. May 2011

Van, Carl. "How to Say No the Right Way." OTC Beauty Magazine. July 2011

Van, Carl. "Gaining Cooperation Three Maxims for Successful Negotiation." The Industry Source. July/August 2011

Van, Carl "Negotiation – Understanding the Other Point of View." Promotional Consultant Today. www.promotionalconsultanttoday.org April 2011

Van, Carl "Gaining Cooperation."
The Minnesota News, June 2011. Pg. 13.
Sales and Service Excellence Magazine, May 2011, Pg. 12.
InSite Magazine. May/June 2011, Vol. 25, No. 6, pg. 10.
Audiology Advance Magazine. www.audiology.advanceweb.com April 2011
Pharmacy Week. www.pharmacyweek.com April 2011
Print Wear Magazine. www.printwearmag.com April 2011
The Real Estate Professional Magazine. www.therealestatepro.com April 2011
Weekly Article Magazine. www.WeeklyArticle.com March 2011.
Industrial Supply Magazine. www.industrialsupplymagazine.com March 2011.
Furniture World Magazine. www.Furninfo.com March 2011.

Contact Professional. www.contactProfessional.com March 2011.

Promotional Consultants Today. www.PromotionalConsultantToday.org; March 2011.

Van, Carl "Three Maxims for Successful Negotiation." Dealer Marketing Magazine www.DealerMarketing.com March 2011.

Van, Carl. "Our Life's Work." Property Casualty 360. www.PropertyCasualty360.com January 2011.

Van, Carl. "The Five Standards of Great Claims Organizations." Property Casualty 360. www.PropertyCasualty360.com February 2011.

Van, Carl. "Online Claims Training Program Expands: Time Management for Claims added to curriculum." Claims Education Magazine. www.claimseducationmagazine.com Fall 2010.

Van, Carl. "5th Annual Claims Education Conference Earns Superbowl Status." Claims Education Magazine. Summer 2010: Pg. 1.

Van, Carl. "While Others Wait, Bold Companies Invest in Training." Subrogator. Winter 2010: Pg. 102.

Van, Carl. "While Others Wait, Bold Companies Invest in Training Part III." <u>Claims Education Magazine</u>. Spring 2010: Pg. 1.

Van, Carl. "Claims Education Conference and the Superbowl Champs." <u>Claims Education Magazine</u>. Spring 2010

Van, Carl. "Customer Service and the Claims Professional." <u>Claims</u>. December 2010

Van, Carl. "A New Season Awaits." <u>Property Casualty 360°</u>. July 2009

Van, Carl. "Welcome to Our Launch." <u>Property Casualty 360°</u>. July 2009

Van, Carl. "While Others Wait, Bold Companies Invest in Training Part II." <u>Claims Education Magazine</u>. December 2009- Vol. 6, No. 6: Pg. 1.

Van, Carl. "While Others Wait, Some Invest in Training." <u>Claims Education Magazine.</u> October/November 2009- Vol. 6, No. 5: Pg. 3

Van, Carl. "Tips on Taking Statements & Information Gathering." <u>Claims Education Magazine.</u> October/November 2009- Vol. 6, No. 5: Pg. 1.

Van, Carl. "Hiring and Motivating the Right People." NASP Daily News. November 2009

Van, Carl. "Placing the Bets." Claims Education Magazine. March/April 2009- Vol. 6, No. 2: Pg. 1.

Van, Carl. "Lessons in Customer Service & Attitude." Claims Education Magazine. January/February 2009- Vol. 6, No. 1: Pg. 1.

Van, Carl. "Saying It the Right Way." Claims Education Magazine. Fall 2008- Vol. 5, No. 4: Pg. 8.

Van, Carl. "Critical Thinking Part Three." Claims Education Magazine. Summer 2008- Vol. 5, No. 3: Pg. 4.

Van, Carl. "Critical Thinking Part Two." Claims Education Magazine. Spring 2008- Vol. 5, No. 2: Pg. 4.

Van, Carl. "Critical Thinking Part One." Claims Education Magazine. Winter 2008- Vol. 5, No. 1: Pg. 4.

Van, Carl. "Desire for Excellence." Claims Education Magazine. Fall 2007- Vol. 4, No. 4: Pg. 14.

Van, Carl. "Above All Else: There is Attitude." Claims Education Magazine. Winter 2006

Van, Carl, "Meeting the Challenges of Time Management." <u>Claims Education Magazine</u>. Summer 2006

Van, Carl. "Building a Claim Team." <u>Claims</u>. October 2005.

Van, Carl. "In Search of Initiative." <u>Claims</u>. September 2005.

Van, Carl. "A Velvet Hammer Can Expedite Negotiations." <u>Claims Education Magazine</u>. Summer 2005- Vol. 1, No. 1: Pg. 10.

Van, Carl. "Claims Management: Desire for Excellence." <u>Claims</u>. July 2005.

Van, Carl. "Empathizing with Customers." <u>Claims</u>. June 2005.

Van, Carl. "Never Stop Learning." <u>Claims</u>. May 2005.

Van, Carl. "Interpersonal Skills: Avoid the Hammer." <u>Claims</u>. April 2005.

Van, Carl. "Secrets of Successful Time Management." <u>Claims</u>. March 2005.

Van, Carl. "Attitude." <u>Claims Magazine</u>. February 2005: Pg. 10.

Van, Carl. "Secrets of Successful Time Management." <u>Claims Magazine</u>. March 2005

Van, Carl. "Adjusters Can Steer Clear of Headaches by Avoiding the Hammer." <u>Claims Education Magazine</u>. Summer 2005

Van, Carl. "Tend to Your Garden: A Vision of Claims Education." <u>Claims.</u> February 2003: Pg. 34.

Van, Carl. "Adjusters: How not to Drive Away Clients." <u>National Underwriter</u>. September 24, 2001.

Van, Carl. "Adjusters Should Holster 'The Hammer'." <u>National Underwriter</u>. November 2001

Van, Carl & Sue Tarrach. "The 8 Characteristics of Awesome Adjusters." <u>Claims.</u> December 1996.

Carl Van is available for consulting, training and guest speaking appearances. To contact Mr. Van, call 504-393-4570 or visit:

www.CarlVan.org

AWESOME CLAIMS CUSTOMER SERVICE

www.Facebook.com/CarlVanSpeaker

www.Linkedin.com/CarlVan (Carl Van - Awesome Adjuster group)

ARTICLES FEATURING CARL VAN

Mr. Van has been the subject of numerous articles outlining his services and educational philosophy. A few are:

DeWitt, Margaret. "Make Sure Your Reps Understand That Their Job is Helping Customers." The Customer Communicator. September 2011

DeWitt, Margaret. "Does Your Attitude Toward Your Job Need Adjusting?" The Customer Communicator. September 2011

Couretas, Catherine. "Maximize Your Employee Training, Performance." International Association of Special Investigation Units. September 2011

Bramlet, Christina. "Speaking of Gaining Cooperation with Carl Van." Claims. April 2011, Vol. 59, pg. 8. Property Casualty 360. www.PropertyCasualty360.com. April 2011

Gilkey, Eric. "Strategies for Gaining Cooperation." IASIU. Monday, September 13, 2010: Pg. 4.

Henry, Susan, and Mary Anne Medina. "Evaluating Adjuster Performance." Claims. August 2010: Pg. 36.

Gilkey, Eric. "Hiring and Motivating the Right People." NASP Daily News, November 3, 2009: Pg. 6.

Gilkey, Eric. "Ace Awards: Most Dynamic Speaker." Claims. July 2009, Vol. 57, No. 57, Pg. 6.

"Permission to Say, 'I'm Sorry." Canadian Underwriter. September 1, 2008.

Aznoff, Dan. "Fair Oaks Students Take Speaker's Advice to Heart for Positive Attitude." The Sacramento Bee. April 12, 2007: City Section, Pg. G5.

Friedman, Sam. "WC Claimants 'Not the Enemy,' Trainer says." National Underwriter. September 24, 2001.

Prochaska, Paul. "Awesome Adjusting Revisited: A Return to Customer Service." Claims. February 2000.

Hays, Daniel. "Being Kinder and Gentler Pays Off: Insurance Claims is a Customer Service Business." Claims. December 2000: Pg. 56.

Carl Van is available for consulting, training and guest speaking appearances. To contact Mr. Van, call 504-393-4570 or visit:

www.CarlVan.org

www.Facebook.com/CarlVanSpeaker

www.Linkedin.com/CarlVan (Carl Van - Awesome Adjuster group)

ADDITIONAL BOOKS BY CARL VAN

Van, Carl. The 8 Characteristics of the Awesome Adjuster. Published by Arthur Hardy Enterprises, Inc., ISBN 0-930892-66-6 (Metairie, LA) Copyright © 2005

Van, Carl. Gaining Cooperation: Some Simple Steps to Getting Customers to do What You Want Them to do. Published by International Insurance Institute, Inc., ISBN 1456334107 & 13-9781456334109 (New Orleans, LA) Copyright © 2011

Van, Carl. Attitude, Ability and the 80-20 Rule. Published by International Insurance Institute, Inc., ISBN 1461052947 & 13:9781461052944 (New Orleans, LA) Copyright © 2011

Van, Carl and Hinz, Debra. Gaining Cooperation: 3 Easy Steps to Getting Injured Workers to do What you Want Them to do. Published by International Insurance Institute, Inc., ISBN: 1461104009 & 13:9781461104001 (New Orleans, LA) Copyright © 2011

Van, Carl and Wimsatt, Laura. The Claims Cookbook: A Culinary Guide to Job Satisfaction. Published by International Insurance Institute, Inc., ISBN: 1460976657 & 13:9781460976654 (New Orleans, LA) Copyright © 2011

Van, Carl. The Eight Characteristics of the Awesome Employee: Published Pelican Publishing ISBN: 978-1-4556-1734-0 & 978-1-4556-1735-7 (Gretna, LA) Copyright © 2012

Van, Carl and Headrick, Teresa. Negotiation Skills for the Claims Professional. Published by International Insurance Institute, Inc., ISBN: 1480291412 & 9781480291416 (New Orleans, LA) Copyright © 2013

Carl Van is available for consulting, training and guest speaking appearances. To contact Mr. Van, call 504-393-4570 or visit:

www.CarlVan.org

www.Facebook.com/CarlVanSpeaker

www.Linkedin.com/CarlVan (Carl Van - Awesome Adjuster group)

CONTACT CARL VAN

Carl Van is available for consulting, training and guest speaking appearances. To contact Mr. Van, call 504-393-4570 or find him at any of the following:

www.InsuranceInstitute.com

www.ClaimsEducationConference.net

www.CarlVan.org

www.ClaimsEducationMagazine.com

www.Facebook.com/CarlVanSpeaker

www.ClaimsEducationOnLine.com

www.Twitter.com/CarlVanSpeaker

www.ClaimsProfessionalBooks.com

www.Linkedin.com (Carl Van – Awesome Adjuster group)

AWESOME CLAIMS CUSTOMER SERVICE

www.YouTube.com/CarlVanTV

www.CarlVanClaimsExpert.wordpress.com

FREQUENTLY ASKED QUESTIONS

This section provides answers to questions Carl frequently gets from those who take my *Exceptional Claims Customer Service* course.

When dealing with an angry customer, why don't you just use the three steps for negotiating for cooperation?

The reason we have separate steps for angry customers is because usually when customers are angry, it's because they wanted something they didn't get. You have to calm them down long enough to help them. The steps when dealing with angry customers help calm them down, especially when you use the apology and refocus steps. Then you can find out what went wrong and see if you can help.

The three steps for negotiating for cooperation are used when you're trying to get the customer to do something. And those are really two separate things. We wouldn't intermingle them.

What do you suggest doing with the customer who does not respond to the three steps for negotiating for cooperation?

As we mentioned before, you can't make someone cooperate. The best you can do is show how you can help if they do cooperate. If somebody never gets to that point, rather than pull out the claims hammer, you should apologize for the fact you can't help them now and ask them to please consider cooperating. Then perhaps they can call you back or you can call them back at an appropriate time.

Why is it that nail down questions don't work to influence people to change their minds? You're getting them to say yes.

It's true that one of the benefits of nail down questions, when you get them to say yes, is that it puts them in the mood for agreement. But that's probably not enough to overcome some objection the customer may have. We would stick to using nail down questions to get them to remember what you say. Then use the three steps for negotiating for cooperation to convince them you're right.

Will these techniques work all of the time? And if not, well then, why use them?

No technique will work one hundred percent of the time. These techniques are very, very valuable most of the time. The vast majority of the customers you deal with will appreciate the fact you acknowledge their point of view rather than hit them over the head with the claims hammer. Will they work all of the time? No. But a good eighty, ninety, ninety-five percent of the time, they are very effective and that's better than not working any of the time. So, use them. Use them the best that you can. Don't expect one hundred percent success. Nothing is one hundred percent successful. But you know what, being successful ninety-five percent of the time is a whole world better than being successful only thirty percent of the time.

I already have way too much work to do in order to even get done at the end of the day. How can I possibly now spend more time using these techniques?

The answer to this one is very simple. All the techniques we have talked about should save you time. They are designed to make the claims job easier. It should save you time when a customer is listening to what you say and remembering what you told them. That should save you phone calls later. It should save you time to show a customer you understand their point of view rather than convince them they're wrong. Put these techniques in place—they don't all have to be put in place at one time—and watch yourself save time during the day.

I have heard co-workers actually call customers names as you've described. What should I do?

Rather than answer this directly, we are going to encourage you to go to www.claimseducationmagazine.com. There's an article called *Who's Picking Up The Claims Trash*? It was written by Ken Sanders and in it, he does an outstanding job of outlining this very situation. We have a responsibility to help each other, especially when it comes to customer service.

We've learned so much in this customer service class, how can we do it all?

Our suggestion is you don't try. You can't possibly break fifteen, twenty, maybe twenty-five habits all at the same time. These are all separate habits we have regarding how we deal with customers. Our suggestion is to pick the top two, maybe three, maybe four and focus on those. Get those working for you and put those into place before you try to move on to the others.

What's the best way to make sure that I don't start slipping back into my bad habits?

For this, we have a couple of suggestions. The first one, and the most important, is to check in with your supervisor or manager. Let them know you are serious, and you want to try to put these skills in place. See if they would be willing to help you role play or maybe monitor your phone calls and give you suggestions later on.

The second one is to seek out a co-worker—maybe someone else who has also read this book—and see if you can use him or her to practice role playing or if you can listen in on each other's phone calls and maybe give each other feedback.

This is the third insurance company I've worked for and I've never seen these skills ever taught before. How is it possible that these things work, yet nobody else knows about them?

The only way we can really answer this question is to reference Dick Fosbury. Dick Fosbury, as some of you may know, was a high jumper. Until Dick Fosbury came along, everybody was jumping over the bar a certain way. Then suddenly Dick Fosbury came along and started jumping over the bar backwards, and they called it the Fosbury Flop. Until Dick Fosbury came along, nobody was jumping over the bar backwards. Now, years later, every person in competition in high jump does the Fosbury Flop. Nobody does it any other way.

Imagine when Dick Fosbury was first using his technique. If he was trying to convince other people that his approach worked, what would he have faced? He would have faced people saying they had never seen that before, my coach has never seen that before, my teammates have never seen that before. How can it possibly work?

The point is just because you haven't seen something before, doesn't mean it doesn't work. Here's a suggestion: Be the Dick Fosbury in your office. Don't wait for somebody else to put these techniques in place. You be the leader who puts them in place and let everybody follow you.

If I am asked to explain the important thing I learned by reading this book, what should that be?

Our guess is that everyone is going to have a different answer to this question. If it were up to us, we would say the overriding theme of this book is that we work in claims to help people. To be an outstanding claims person means to be an outstanding customer service provider—someone who understands that we are here to help.

Who should I contact or what should I do if I have a question about anything in this course?

The International Insurance Institute has technical experts that can answer your questions. Another option is to send Carl a personal e-mail. His e-mail address is carlvan@insuranceinstitute.com. He would be more than happy to answer any question you might have.

Made in the USA
Middletown, DE
05 October 2022